James Stevenson Riggs

Outline Studies in the Gospel of John

prepared for the Rhode Island Committee of Pastors

James Stevenson Riggs

Outline Studies in the Gospel of John
prepared for the Rhode Island Committee of Pastors

ISBN/EAN: 9783337381592

Printed in Europe, USA, Canada, Australia, Japan

Cover: Foto ©Lupo / pixelio.de

More available books at **www.hansebooks.com**

Outline Studies in the Gospel of John,

BY

JAMES STEVENSON RIGGS, D. D.,

Professor of Biblical Criticism in Auburn Theological Seminary, Auburn, N. Y.

Prepared for the Rhode Island Committee of Pastors.

The aim of these outline studies is by analysis, suggestion and question to direct and stimulate work upon this great gospel. All helps to New Testament study must be more or less mechanical. Individual, personal, meditative, devout attention will with guidance secure the best results. It is to afford guidance to such attention that these outlines are prepared.

LITERATURE.

For critical work: Reynolds, Godet, Westcott, Dods (in Expositor's Greek Testament, Vol. I) and Luthardt. For work which seeks an understanding of the gospel without such close, critical study as the above commentaries require: Dods (Expositor's Bible—John); Maurice, the Gospel of John. For work on the Johannine Problem: the New Testament Introductions of Weiss, Salmon, Gloag and Watkin's Bampton Lectures for 1890 together with introductions found in the critical commentaries cited. Valuable help will also be gained from Weiss's, Edersheim's or Andrews' Life of Christ.

Outline Study 1.

CHAPTER I.

Introductory. As preparatory to our study the following considerations are of especial importance. 1. *The purpose of the gospel given* (20:31). This purpose has controlled the selection of material and has dominated the plan of the gospel. It is well, therefore, to know it accurately and to keep it in mind as we study each section. 2. *The great divisions of the gospel.* Each of these while holding to the main purpose, viz.: the manifestation of Jesus as the Messiah emphasizes the acceptance or rejection of that manifestation. There are five divisions,—Chapters I–IV, V–XII, XIII–XVII, XVIII–XIX, XX (XXI).

THE PROLOGUE.

I. Analysis: Theme, *The Logos.*

  I. The Preexistent Logos.

His relations $\begin{cases} \text{to God, 1, 2.} \\ \text{to creation, 3.} \\ \text{to men, 4, 5.} \end{cases}$

  II. The Logos in History.

  (*a*) Point of view for contemplating this, 6, 7, 8.
  (*b*) Where the Logos manifested Himself.
    1. In conscience, 9, 10.
    2. In special revelations to the Jews.
    3. In incarnate form, 11.
  (*c*) The deepening darkness of unbelief in view of these manifestations.

  III. The Logos Incarnate.

  (*a*) His visible glory, 14.
  (*b*) His abounding fulness, 16.
  (*c*) His interpretation to us of the Father, 18.
  (*d*) The blessedness of faith in view of these manifestations.

II. Suggestions and Questions for Study. 1. In view of what heresy is the teaching of the first section formed? 2. What is *exactly* the teaching of the first section of the prologue? 3. Why in verse 4 does John say "in Him *was* life"? 4. Explain how "life is light?" 5. In the historic summary of 6-13 why is the beginning made with John the Baptist? 6. What is the exact meaning of "true" in John's gospel? 7. Would you put "coming into the world" (v. 9) in connection with "man" or "light"? 8. What is the Johannine meaning of the verb "to know"? 9. How should you understand v. 12? What light does it throw upon the modern teaching that all men are sons of God? 10. Why the threefold negation in verse 13? 11. What is the meaning of "glory" in verse 14? 12. Just what is meant by "grace and truth" (v. 14) and "grace for grace" (v. 16)?

13. Draw out all you can of what is involved in the antithesis of verse 17. 14. Give your idea of the Son's interpretation of the Father. 15. Write out a paraphrase of verses 1-18. 16. There are three great facts of the experience of Jesus set forth in this prologue; what are they?

III. **Copics for Research.** 1. The history of the term "the Word." (See Introductions to critical commentaries; Hastings' Bible Dictionary, "Logos"; Stevens' Johannine Theology, pp. 75-101.) 2. The use of the term "flesh" in the New Testament. (See Hastings' Bible Dictionary; Laidlaw's Bible Doctrine of Man.) 3. Compare carefully the doctrine of Christ taught in this section with Phil. 2:6-11; Col. 1:15-20; 2:9; Heb. 1:1-3.

THE BEGINNINGS OF THE HISTORY.

Consistent with his purpose John does not begin his account of Jesus until after the Temptation. He wishes us to come face to face with Him who was given His mission at the Baptism and made clear and sure of the way of its realization by the Temptation. He is the Messiah indeed now who steps out into the light of public service. He is equipped with power and ready to begin His work. It is clearly part of John's plan to begin just at this point. What the synoptics have given us of times and events before this would not have answered his purpose. It is the Messiah — proclaimed, tried, triumphant — whom John wishes us to see. It would be well to get clearly in mind the events which John has passed over. By keeping the Johannine account in relation to the synoptic, we shall the more clearly see how the fourth gospel unfolds its plan.

IV. **Analysis** of 1:19-51.

Testimonials to Jesus and the Awakening of Faith.

A. First Testimony: John the Baptist and the Jews, 19-28.
   (*a*) Occasion of it, 19.
   (*b*) Questions answered by it, 20, 25.
   (*c*) Its fruitlessness and the general analogy of this whole scene to the movement of the prologue. Trace this.

B. Second Testimony: John and Jesus, 29-34.
   (*a*) Occasion of it, 29.
   (*b*) The twofold import of it. Mark this.
   (*c*) The place of John's Baptism and the relation of the Baptism of the Spirit to the taking away of sin, 32, 33.
   (*d*) The peculiar import of the phrase "Son of God," 34.

C. Third Testimony: John, Jesus, and Disciples, 34-44.
   (*a*) Occasion of it, 35.
   (*b*) The response of Andrew and John, 37, 40.
   (*c*) The results of that response, 41.
   (*d*) The prophecy which involved the secret of successful discipleship, 42.

D. Fourth Testimony: Jesus and Nathaniel, 45-51.

   (*a*) Occasion of it, 45-48.

   (*b*) The peculiar promise given in response to it, 51.

U. Suggestions and Questions for Study. 1. Get exactly the facts which will fill out the subdivisions of the analysis. 2. How is the phrase "the Jews" used in John? 3. Give the historical explanation for the questions asked, 20-21. 4. What was the chief interest of Jerusalem in John the Baptist? 5. Was baptism a common rite among the Jews? 6. Study carefully the three stages of the preaching of John the Baptist as given in Matt. 3 : 12 and Luke 3 : 1-18; John 1 : 29-34; John 3 : 23-36. Get the themes of each stage and show the change of tone in this section. 7. How much is involved in the geographical statement " Bethany beyond Jordan "? 8. To what "Lamb" does John refer in v. 29? 9. In what sense did John not know Jesus? 10. What do you think was involved in this Baptism of the Spirit upon Jesus? 11. How does John reckon time, e. g. in speaking of the tenth hour? 12. Give all the facts out of these narratives which go to show that John, the evangelist, was one of the newly-found disciples. 13. How much do you put into the phrase "we have found the Messiah"? Try to get the exact historical situation here. 14. What is the force of the prophecy of Jesus "thou shalt be called Cephas"? 15. Where was the Bethsaida of verse 44? 16. Does Jesus go to Galilee to begin his public ministry there? 17. Do we ever hear of Nathaniel in the gospels after this time? 18. Show that in his question of surprise (v. 46) Nathaniel did not mean to slander Nazareth. 19. Can you give any plausible reason why Jesus said to Nathaniel just what He did when He met him? 20. Compare Nathaniel's declaration in v. 50 with the description of Melchisedek in Heb. 7 : 1-3. 21. Did Nathaniel have any fulfillment of the promise made to him in verse 51? Show the possibility of it from what you know of the life of Jesus. 22. Do the words of Jesus to Nathaniel show a miracle of omniscience?

UI. Topics for Research. 1. The Pharisees: What was their political position? What were their chief religious tenets? How did they conceive of the Messiah? (See Hastings' Bible Dictionary; Schürer's Jewish People in the Time of Christ, Div. II, Vol. II; Edersheim's Life of Christ, Vol. I.) 2. The Baptism of John; its origin and peculiar character. (See Hastings' Bible Dictionary; Reynolds' John the Baptist.) 3. The Son of Man: the origin of the phrase and its use by Jesus. (See Bruce, Kingdom of God, p. 166; Stevens' Theology of the New Testament, p. 41 ; Wendt, Teaching of Jesus, Vol. II, p. 139.)

Outline Studies in the Gospel of John,

BY

JAMES S. RIGGS, D. D.,

Professor of Biblical Criticism in Auburn Theological Seminary, Auburn, N. Y.

Prepared for the Rhode Island Committee of Pastors.

The aim of these outline studies is by analysis, suggestion and question to direct and stimulate work upon this great gospel. All helps to New Testament study must be more or less mechanical. Individual, personal, meditative, devout attention will with guidance secure the best results. It is to afford guidance to such attention that these outlines are prepared.

LITERATURE.

For critical work: Reynolds, Godet, Westcott, Dods (in Expositor's Greek Testament, Vol. I) and Luthardt. For work which seeks an understanding of the gospel without such close, critical study as the above commentaries require: Dods (Expositor's Bible—John); Maurice, the Gospel of John. For work on the Johannine Problem: the New Testament Introductions of Weiss, Salmon, Gloag and Watkin's Bampton Lectures for 1890 together with introductions found in the critical commentaries cited. Valuable help will also be gained from Weiss's, Edersheim's or Andrews' Life of Christ.

Outline Study II.

CHAPTER II

The Testimony of Signs. Cana's Miracle, the Cleansing of the Temple. and other signs in Jerusalem.

I. The First Sign: Testimony to Power. The Miracle at Cana. (1-11.)

    1. The two significant moments in the story :

        (*a*) The request of Mary and the answer of Jesus. (3-4.)

        (*b*) The actual change or water to wine. (5-10.)

    2. The point of John's comment. (11.)

II. Suggestions and Questions for Study.

    1. What were the probable reasons for the journey to Cana?

    2. What third day is referred to? (2.)

    3. What two sites have been defended as the locations for ancient Cana? Which do you accept and why?

    4. Give an account of a Jewish wedding in Christ's time. (See Edersheim : " Sketches of Jewish Social Life," pp. 138-160. especially p. 151).

    5. Paraphrase the question of Jesus (4) so as to relieve it of all harshness.

    6. To what " hour " does Jesus refer? (See John 7 : 30 ; 8 : 20 : 12 : 23, 27 ; 13 : 1 ; 17 : 1).

    7. What bearing has the statement " mine hour has not yet come" upon the question?

    8. Christ's answer to his Mother implies far more in her request than appears in her actual words. To get at this implication, review the recent scenes at the Jordan, the annunciation to Mary, (Luke 1 : 28-33) and try to get Mary's point of view.

    9. Godet compares Mary's request to the third form of the Temptation in the Wilderness (Luke 4 : 9): show the resemblance.

    10. How much water would six water pots hold?

    11. Would you agree with Westcott that only that amount of water which the servants carried to the ruler of the feast was changed to wine?

    12. Was this such wine as could intoxicate, if taken in large quantities?

    13. If so, how do you justify Jesus in producing it?

    14. What is the peculiar significance of the word " sign " as descriptive of a miracle?

    15. What other terms are used in the New Testament to describe miracles? Give the force of each.

    16. Just how does this miracle manifest the glory of Jesus?

17. How would you meet the objection that it is "a useless miracle?"

18. Show the relationship of the miracle to the purpose of John's Gospel.

III. Topics for Research. 1. Miracles. The supernatural is in our day seriously questioned. It should, therefore, have careful attention. The Miracles beget questions regarding evidence and questions in philosophy. The following literature will be found helpful in studying this important subject: Bruce, "The Miraculous Element in the Gospels"; Hastings' B D article, Miracle, by Bernard; Mozley, on Miracles; Taylor, "The Gospel Miracles in their Relation to Christ and Christianity"; Weiss, "Life of Christ" vol. II : 98 ff.: Fairbairn, "Studies in the Life of Christ," pp. 149-164, 197-218.

IU. The Second Sign. Testimony to Authority.

The Cleansing of the Temple. (13-22.)

1. The time of this first public act. (13.)
2. The occasion of it. (14, 16.)
3. The method of it. (15.)
4. The effect of it. (11, 13.)
5. The attitude of the Jews and the word of Jesus. (18-20.)
6. The comment of the Evangelist. (21, 22.)

With this startling scene in the Temple, John opens the public ministry of Jesus. The Fourth Gospel knows nothing of any earlier visit to Jerusalem than this. It is well to bear in mind, however, how completely the position of Jesus toward the holy city was changed by all that occurred at the Baptism. Jesus comes now to Jerusalem as the Messiah. He performs an act which is symbolic of his great mission. His cleansing of the Central Shrine of the nation is truly Messianic. Hence we believe that this scene at the opening of the ministry is certainly in its right place. If one were called upon to decide between John and the Synoptics, only one cleansing being allowed, the decision should be for John's order as regards this narrative. (See Weiss, "Life of Christ," vol. I : p. 387 ff.)

U. Suggestions and Questions for Study.

1. In order to the full appreciation of this scene try to get the outlook of Jesus as given in Luke 41 : 50, and then estimate the bearing of the Baptism and the Temptation upon the thought of the Master.

2. Give a description of Herod's Temple. (Read Josephus Antiquities, XV : 11; Jewish War, V : 5; and see Hastings' B D article, Temple, vol. IV : 711).

3. Account for the traffic in the Temple Courts.

4. Had Jesus any legal right to cause this disturbance? Who had the Temple in charge?

5. Paraphrase verse 17 so as to give its full meaning.

6. Paul says that "the Jews ask for signs." (1 Cor. 1:22.) Give the reason for this mental attitude and explain its appearance in this scene.

7. Is it an objection that we have here so early a reference by Jesus himself to his death? Note carefully where the first reference to the same issue appears in the Synoptics.

8. Jesus says "*my* Father's house." How much is involved in the possessive "*my*"? Does Jesus ever identify himself with the disciples in a petition or reference to the Father? (Classify the varying instances by using a Concordance upon the word Father).

9. How do you harmonize an undoubted reference to the Temple in v. 19 with John's explanation in v. 21?

10. What Scripture is referred to in v. 22.

11. Show as fully as you can how this section furthers the plan of John.

UI. Topics for Research.

1. Compare carefully this account with Mark 11:15-18, in order to answer this question: "Were there two cleansings of the Temple or only one?" (See Andrews' "Life of Our Lord," 167-170; Weiss, "Life of Christ," vol. II:3-17; Edersheim, "Life and Times of Jesus," vol. I:364-374).

2. Give the number, order, time and significance of the Jewish feasts. John's Gospel has been called "the Gospel of the Feasts." It is, therefore, helpful to have definite information regarding them. An excellent account of them will be found ih Edersheim's "The Temple, its Ministries and Services." See also Hasting's, B D vol. I, Feasts.

3. In verse 12 it is said that "his brethren" went down with Jesus to Capernaum. See Matt. 1:25, and Luke 2:7 and acquaint yourself with the discussion connected with this relationship. (See Godet, John, vol. II:20-25; Hastings, B D vol. I:p. 320).

UII. Other Signs. Testimonies to the Power and Person of Christ. (23-25.)

1. The faith they inspired. (23.)

2. The bearing of Jesus toward that faith and the reason for that bearing. (24.)

3. The whole outcome of this witness of signs.

UIII. Suggestions and Questions for Study.

1. What do you understand by the phrase "believing on his name?"

2. What is the distinguishing mark of vital faith?

3. What element failed in·the sign-born faith?

4. Generally verse 25 is explained by postulating supernatural knowledge on the part of Jesus. Try to give an adequate explanation without introducing the supernatural.

5. Give in full the outcome of these testimonies of signs.

6. What sign is required today in order to believe in Christ?

Outline Studies in the Gospel of John,

BY

JAMES S. RIGGS, D. D.,

Professor of Biblical Criticism in Auburn Theological Seminary, Auburn, N. Y.

Prepared for the Rhode Island Committee of Pastors.

The aim of these outline studies is by analysis, suggestion and question to direct and stimulate work upon this great gospel. All helps to New Testament study must be more or less mechanical. Individual, personal, meditative, devout attention will with guidance secure the best results. It is to afford guidance to such attention that these outlines are prepared.

LITERATURE.

For critical work: Reynolds, Godet, Westcott, Dods (in Expositor's Greek Testament, Vol. I) and Luthardt. For work which seeks an understanding of the gospel without such close, critical study as the above commentaries require: Dods (Expositor's Bible—John); Maurice, the Gospel of John. For work on the Johannine Problem: the New Testament Introductions of Weiss, Salmon, Gloag and Watkin's Bampton Lectures for 1890 together with introductions found in the critical commentaries cited. Valuable help will also be gained from Weiss's, Edersheim's or Andrews' Life of Christ.

Outline Study III.

The Conversation with Nicodemus and the Comments of John.

Introductory. Jesus has already manifested Himself by *deeds* such as the miracle at Cana and the cleansing of the temple. We are now to study a manifestation of His Messianic glory in his words. This is the first of the eleven discourses which really make the Gospel of John. Several features of these discourses are noteworthy. 1. They contain, for the most part, only the great themes of the Master's addresses. The connection often lies beneath the surface and can be gained only by a full knowledge of the situation and by reflection. 2. They are all in John's style. This is due partly to the fact that they are translations; partly to the fact that they come to us through the medium of John's reflection. They are none the less true. As Matthew Arnold has said, "the doctrine and discourses of Jesus *cannot* in the main be the writer's, because in the main they are clearly out of his reach." There *is* an element of subjectivity in the Fourth Gospel. 3. These addresses are almost entirely given to those who have been educated either in the Jewish schools or by an exceptional experience. The conversation with the Samaritan woman is an exception. The above characteristics go a long way in meeting the critical objections made to these discourses.

The conversation with Nicodemus is very brief. To get at its connections and import one should study (*a*) the religious situation in Jerusalem; (*b*) the hopes of the Jews in regard to the Messianic Kingdom. (See Schürer, Jewish People in the Time of Christ: Pharisees, Sadducees, Scribes, Synagogue, and the same articles in Hastings' Bib. Dict. Also, Drummond's The Jewish Messiah and the article, Messiah, in Hastings' B. D.)

The Conversation with Nicodemus.

I. Analysis of 3 : 1-15.

    1. The occasion of it:

        (*a*) The " we know " of the awakened teacher, 2.

        (*b*) His questioning earnestness about the kingdom. (See question 6 below.)

    2. Its two-fold division:

        (*a*) Earthly things e. g. entering the kingdom.

            (1) The peculiar significance of the figure used in v. 3.

            (2) The singular combination of means, 5.

            (3) The inner meaning of the fact itself, 6.

        (*b*) Heavenly things.

            (1) His right and ability to speak of them, 11-13.

            (2) The condition indispensable to being able to enter the kingdom, 14, 15.

II. Suggestions and Questions for Study.

    1. With what in the preceding context does this scene have connection? 2. How much is involved in the description "a ruler of the Jews"? 3. Note that the statement (v. 2) is "*we* know;" why "we?" 4. Estimate the action of the Pharisees in Matt. 12 : 22-45 in the light of this confession from a Pharisee. It helps one to see why they were in

danger of "eternal sin." 5. Between verses 5 and 6 there is a gap in the conversation shown by the abrupt change. Fill in the gap. We would suggest for this: an inquiry on the part of Nicodemus about the kingdom—its nature and his relation to it. Before filling in the gap in this way, ascertain the views of the ruling classes upon the subject. (See literature given above and Prof. Charles' Eschatology Jewish and Christian.) 6. Christ's answer has been variously translated "except a man be born 'anew,' 'again' or 'from above.'" Study carefully the whole conversation to see whether you can accept the translation of the R. V. (See also additional note in Westcott, p. 63.) 7. Is the question of Nicodemus in v. 4 serious or is it made simply to draw out Jesus? 8. Study in the second reply of Jesus the means "water and spirit." The only interpretation of this which is correct is to be gained from the historical situation. What in that situation led Jesus to combine "water" and "spirit?" 9. Is the statement in v. 10 the word of Jesus or a comment of the evangelist? Give any possible reasons for the latter view. Also paraphrase the statement so as to give its exact force. 10. There are two possible translations of v. 8. Give the reasons for each and for your preference. (For a compact, clear discussion see the Cambridge Bible for Schools—John, in loco.) 11. In the original of the last clause of v. 8 a Greek perfect is used. If you know Greek, bring out the complete and exact meaning of this clause. 12. Just what is it in the word of Jesus which puzzles Nicodemus? 13. Show, if you can, from the Old Testament and from contemporary Jewish teaching that Nicodemus ought not to have been puzzled. 14. Mark, also, what a revelation of the spiritual incompetency of the teachers in Israel this perplexity of Nicodemus is! 15. Does Jesus ever use what we call an editorial "we" or what some commentators describe as a "plural of majesty?" Look through the discourses before you answer and explain the "we" of v. 11. 16. When Jesus says, "we are bearing witness to what we have seen," what does He mean? 17. One of the difficult words of this discourse is the description "earthly." Illustrate it from His teaching. The doctrine of this conversation seems wonderfully spiritual. 18. Show the connection between 12 and 13. 19. Does v. 13 imply the incarnation and *preëxistence?* 19. One of the "heavenly things" is given us in v. 14; what is it?

III. Topics for Research.

1. The conditions given in this gospel for entrance into the Kingdom of Heaven, or, (what is the equivalent in the Fourth Gospel), the conditions for obtaining eternal life. (Use a concordance upon the word "life.") 2. Christ's knowledge of His death. Did He come to it gradually as opposition developed or did He know from the beginning that He must die on the cross? To one who postulates the omniscience of Jesus, such a question is already answered, but it is well to remember that very different explanations have been given to v. 14 of this chapter. Read Weiss, Life of Christ, in connection with such passages as 2:19; 3:14, etc.

Comments of the Evangelist.

We come here for the first time upon a feature of this gospel which deserves thoughtful attention. It is to be remembered that John wrote long after the time of the events here recorded. The author looked back upon the life and teaching of his Master from the point of view of the end of the century. Paul's splendid work had been accomplished and his theology of the crucifixion and resurrection had been written. The whole meaning of the incarnation had been set forth. The nature, power and reach of the Messiahship of Jesus were understood. It was possible, therefore, for the evangelist to add where he thought it necessary such comment upon the words of Christ as would give their full significance. In so doing he has made the words of Jesus the basis of all the reflections he has written. He writes such comments not upon his own authority, but as the result of a profound insight into the character and mission of Jesus. Comments of this kind are found in vs. 16-21. Both the character of the statements and the phraseology show that we have here the words of John rather than those of the Savior. It is but fair to say that this is not the conclusion of all who have studied these verses. See Westcott for one view and Godet for the opposite. Weigh the evidence on both sides and seek to reach your own conclusion.

TU. Analysis of 3:16-21. The Mission of the Son.

    1. Its source and purpose.
        (*a*) Source—The love of God, 16.
        (*b*) Purpose—to give life through faith—to save the world, 16, 17.
    2. The consequences attending it.
        (*a*) No judgment for him who believes, 18.
        (*b*) Judgment upon unbelief.
        The reasons for these consequences.
            (1) The love of darkness on one side since deeds are evil, 19, 20.
            (2) The love of light since one does the truth, 21.

U. Suggestions and Questions for Study.

    1. Note that giving is the measure as well as the result of love. The verb translated "loved" in this verse always involves an act of the will. 2. Can you give the inner reason (according to scripture) why faith brings eternal life? 3. What does "eternal" mean in this connection? A better translation is possible; can you give it? 4. Give the different meanings of "world" in the N. T. 5. Just what does it mean "to believe in the name of"? 6. Paraphrase v. 19 so as to bring out its full force. Avoid figurative language in so doing. 7. The word "hate" is the opposite of the verb "love;" it, therefore, also points to an attitude of will. (See Matt. 6:24; Luke 14:26.) 8. Which is the more accurate expression of the thought in v. 21, "that they have been wrought in God" or "*because* they have been wrought in God"? 9. This brief section (19-21) is worthy of study as presenting the innermost reason for indifference to the spiritual on one side and joy in it on the other.

UT. Topics for Research.

    John's Doctrine of Judgment. In order to this study, gather together (with the help of a concordance) all the passages in the gospel pertaining to judgment. Classify them and form a doctrine by the inductive method. See also Stevens' Johannine Theology, pp. 346-354. In all questions of eschatology in John note how far *process* is emphasized as against apocalyptic scenes such as are given in Matt. 25:31-46 and Rev. 20:11-15.

Outline Studies in the Gospel of John,

BY

JAMES STEVENSON RIGGS, D. D.,

Professor of Biblical Criticism in Auburn Theological Seminary, Auburn, N. Y.

Prepared for the Rhode Island Committee of Pastors.

*Outline Study IV.

CHAPTER III : 22 to IV : 42.

JESUS IN JUDEA AND SAMARIA.

A — IN JUDEA.

After the Cleansing of the Temple, the various signs within the city and the Conversation with Nicodemus Jesus left Jerusalem and spent several months in the country districts of Judea. His presentation of Himself in the metropolis had met with little response and it had not yet been shown by that sad indication, the imprisonment of the Baptist, that He should begin His work in Galilee. He still had His desires fixed upon the Capitol and while awaiting His opportunity used the time to make preparation much as John the Baptist himself was doing at Aenon near to Salim. The disciples of Jesus in all probability preached the same message and administered the same rite. For a time the work of the two, of Jesus and of His forerunner, seemed to run parallel and the apparent rivalry in service of the disciples of the Master caused the disciples of John anxiety and dissatisfaction. This feeling gave the Baptist the occasion for his last recorded tribute to his Master to which John appends some profound reflections of his own. It is this tribute which serves the plan of John.

I. The Baptist's Last Testimony. A joyful Recognition of the Master's Supremacy and Enlarging Influence, 29E, 30.

joyful since (*a*)   The positions of all men in honorable service are given them by God. That fact in itself carries high honor with it, 27.

(*b*)   He had always considered himself as the friend of the bridegroom who can only rejoice at the bridegroom's voice, 29.

II. Suggestions and Questions for Study. 1. Give a general picture of "the land of Judea" at this time. 2. What are the data for determining the length of the Lord's sojourn in Judea? 3. Locate Aenon and show that the modern Ainun answers well to the ancient site. (See Conder's Tent Work II : 57, 58.) 4. What is the value of the statement in verse 24? 5. Distinguish Johannine from Christian Baptism. 6. As Jesus did

---

* For Literature, &c., see previous outlines.

not Himself baptize (4:2) suggest some line of activity in which He may have been engaged at this time. 7. Was there an easy possibility of confounding the work of John and Jesus? Prove your answer. 8. In the discussion "about purifying" what was probably the theme? Study the historical situation before answering. 9. Using both the Synoptics and John in order to frame your answer, give the geographical range of the Baptist's preaching. 10. How wide an application would you give the statement of verse 27? 11. How deep down in the nature of things was the "*must*" of verse 30a imbedded?

III. Topic for Research. The Character and Results of the Early Judean Ministry of Jesus up to this time.

COMMENTS OF THE EVANGELIST.

For the same reasons given for the judgment that verses 16-21 of chapter 3 contain the words of the evangelist, these words in 31-36 are to be attributed to the same source. See Westcott on one side and Godet, again, on the other.

IV. Analysis of III: 31-36. The Supremacy of the Son.

      I. By reason of His origin. He is from above and so in contrast to any other teacher who is "of the earth," 31.

      II. By reason of His Teaching. He bears witness to what He hath seen and heard, 32.

          The confirmation which faith gives to the supreme value of this teaching, 33, and the reason, 34.

      III. By reason of His position. All things are given into His hand, 35.

          Conclusion: The consequences to men from the acceptance or rejection of Him who is thus supreme, 36.

V. Suggestions and Questions for Study. 1. Does verse 31 involve the doctrine of preexistence? 2. In this chapter there are three questions in Textual Criticism which merit close attention. They concern verses 13, 15, and 31. (See Westcott on John: Additional note 2 on chapter III.) 3. This short section also presents us with a marked characteristic of John's style, viz: asyndetic statement of thoughts. See for example verses 31-33; 35, 36. In all these verses but one conjunction appears in the original to mark thought relations. These verses, therefore, should be paraphrased in order to bring out the *underlying* connection. Until that can be done one is not sure that he has grasped the connection. 4. Does "of the earth" (31) mean the same as "of the world?" (See 17:14.) 5. Bring out by paraphrase the force of the two "fors" in verse 34. 6. Was John the Baptist historically in a position to make the statement of verse 35? 7. Is the last statement of verse 32 to be absolutely taken? 8. Note the suggestive contrast in verse 36: believeth — hath, etc.; *obeyeth not* — shall not see, etc.

VI. Topics for Research. 1. The relation of the Holy Spirit to service. Does the N. T. teach a baptism for service, as distinct from the presence of the Spirit for Sanctification? 2. Give a clear, careful interpretation of the expression "*the wrath of God.*" (See N. T. Theologies of Weiss and Beyschlag and Stevens' Pauline Theology, p. 99. See also Cremer Biblico—Theo. Lexicon, p. 460, 4th edition.)

The fourth chapter of John has been seriously disputed more than once because of its Samaritan Episode. As preliminary to its study therefore two subjects need careful attention: 1. The Samaritans themselves. Acquaint yourself as fully as possible with their history, their national character and their religious expectations. (See Schürer, Jewish People, Div. II, Vol. I, pp. 5-8; Edersheim's Life of Jesus, Vol. I, pp. 396 ff. and Bible Dictionaries, Samaria and Samaritans.) Particularly in reference to the last theme has the historicity of this chapter been questioned. 2. The work and possible influence of John the Baptist in Samaria. The chapter divides itself naturally into four parts. Of these we shall consider three in this Outline: (1) The conversation of Jesus with the Woman at the Well, (4-26.) (2) The experience of Jesus with the Disciples, (27-38) and (3) The Conduct of the Samaritan Village. As the cure of the Nobleman's son is seemingly but an incident in Galilee the real reason for this departure of Jesus from Judea is given by John, viz: the suspicious, threatening attitude of the Pharisees. We would suggest this chronological arrangement of events: (*a*) Jesus goes toward Galilee for the reason John assigns, (4:1, 2.) (*b*) He journeys through Samaria. (*c*) He arrives at Cana where He cures the Nobleman's son. (*d*) He returns to Jerusalem to the feast (John 5:1) and while there hears of the imprisonment of the Baptist. In consequence He goes again to Galilee, (Matt. 4:12; Mark 1:14.) This order differs from that of Stevens and Burton; it is supported by Andrews. The first division of the chapter constitutes a fine psychological study. Jesus advances by three distinct stages to secure His object.

THE CONVERSATION WITH THE SAMARITAN WOMAN.

1st Advance — to the quickening of her interest, 7-16.
2nd Advance — to the awakening of her conscience, 17-19.
3rd Advance — to the full declaration of Himself, 20-26.
The whole process is worthy of critical and reflective study.

UII. Suggestions and Questions for Study. 1. Make a map of the eastern end of the valley of Schechem locating Sycar, Jacob's Well, Mount Gerizim and Mount Ebal. (See also Smith's Hist. Geog. p. 371.) 2. Give the history of Jacob's Well. 3. What hour was "the *sixth* hour"? 4. Is it true that the Jews went around by the Perea rather than through Samaria when they were bound for Jerusalem from Galilee or, going northward, from Jerusalem for Galilee? (See Josephus Acct. XX: 6, 1.) 5. The relation of knowing, asking and giving in verse 10 is suggestive. A missionary inspiration is in it. 6. Explain the words of Jesus "*living water*" (10); also "the water I shall give him shall become in him a well of water," etc., (14.) 7. Why the sudden turn "go call thy husband"? (16.) 8. Have we in what Jesus tells the woman a miracle of omniscience? 9. Where in the whole account do you find the first trace of a recognition in the woman's mind of deeper meanings than earthly wells of water? 10. Is the question of worship in verse 20 an attempt to slip out from under a personal conviction? 11. Write out in full the doctrine of "ideal worship" as here set forth. First make a critical study of each clause and sentence pertaining to the theme. 12. What does Jesus mean in saying of the Samaritans that they worship that which they know not? (22.) 13. Give reasons for the translation "God is Spirit" rather than "God is a Spirit."

VIII. Topics for Research. 1. From the moment of His Baptism Jesus was conscious of His Messiahship. How did He proceed in the revelation of that consciousness? A correct answer to this question which can be given only after examining carefully the Synoptics and John, will remove a serious objection made to the Johannine narrative. 2. What was the Jewish doctrine of the Fatherhood of God in Christ's time? (See Toy, Judaism and Christianity, Chapter II; Hastings' Bible Dict., Vol. II, p. 208.)

THE EXPERIENCE OF JESUS WITH THE DISCIPLES.

It is a question whether John remained at the well with Jesus. The whole account bespeaks an eye-witness. It is sometimes thought that the question of verse 33 argues against the presence of anyone of the disciples, but it is by no means conclusive. The disciples return from Sychar, are astonished at the twofold disregard on the part of Jesus of Jewish prejudices and elicit from Him the words given in 32, 34-38, which concern

    1. The food of the soul, 32-34.
    2. The Christian Harvest, 35-38.

IX. Suggestions and Questions for Study. 1. Does this expression of Jesus about food throw any light upon the Temptation experience? 2. Note the joy of the Master who though He came to save is yet so deeply touched by the responsiveness of a sinful woman. 3. In verse 34 do the verbs "do" and "finish" refer to *process* or *end*? If you are a student of the Greek, consult the original here before answering. 4. Give the underlying connection between 34-35. (See Westcott.) 5. Show that the words "there are yet four months and then cometh the harvest" do not form a proverb, but are a real indication of time. 6. Give some account of the harvests in Palestine: the time of them in the Jordan plain, in the Shephelah and on the Central ridge; the grain and the method of harvesting. (See Hastings' B. D., Agriculture.) 7. What were the "white fields" which Jesus saw? 8. Paraphrase verses 36, 37 so as to bring out their meaning. 9. To just what is Jesus referring in the statements of verse 38? What labors had they entered into?

THE CONDUCT OF THE SAMARITAN VILLAGE.

In response to the excited, earnest call of the woman, the town seemingly turns out to see this wonderful prophet and a harvest is gathered.

X. Suggestions and Questions for Study. 1. A favorite expression of John in Greek is rendered in English literally "they believed *into* Him." Can you tell why a preposition indicating motion is used? 2. Give the different incitements to faith mentioned in this short section. 3. Do you think that the words "we know that this is indeed the Christ, the Savior of the world" should be attributed to the evangelist, as Weiss declares, or are they the words of the Samaritans? An answer to this should be given only after reflection.

XI. Topics for Research. 1. See Acts VIII : 5, and meet the objection that this account in John leaves no room for the evangelizing work of Philip. 2. Compare in the interests of psychological study, the methods of Jesus with Nicodemus and the Samaritan Woman. What are the fundamental differences of mental attitude, the different problems to be solved by the Master and the results?

Outline Studies in the Gospel of John,

BY

JAMES STEVENSON RIGGS, D. D.,

Professor of Biblical Criticism in Auburn Theological Seminary, Auburn, N. Y.

Prepared for the Rhode Island Committee of Pastors.

*Outline Study V.

JOHN IV : 43 - 54 ; V : 1 - 47.

An Incident in Galilee and the Closing Event of the Early Judean Ministry.

I.

AN INCIDENT IN GALILEE.

THE CURE OF THE NOBLEMAN'S SON.

Introductory. Jesus spent two days with the Samaritans (4 : 40) and then took His departure for Galilee. Why did He go to Galilee? In 4 : 1-3 the reason given is : the suspicious, threatening attitude of the Pharisees. But in verse 44 another reason seems to be given. The critical question regarding this much disputed verse is whether its reason looks to the Galilee into which He was going or to Judea out of which He came. The simpler explanation seems to be that which makes " His own country" refer to Judea. (See, however, Meyer and Godet on one side and Westcott and Reynolds on the other). Any explanation which distinguishes between Nazareth and Galilee or Upper and Lower Galilee is rather forced. Jesus met with a cordial reception from the Galileans, who brought word of His wonderful deeds at the Passover feast, and He visited Cana again. Note how this miracle is referred to—" He came again to Cana " (46). " This is again the second sign that Jesus did having come out of Judea into Galilee." Do not such notes indicate that the real Galilean Ministry had not yet begun?

I. Suggestions and Questions for Study. 1. In what relation does this incident of the miraculous cure stand to the statement of verse 45? 2. Is "nobleman" a good translation? What was probably the official station of this man? 3. What was the relation of Herod Antipas to the Roman Government and what privileges were allowed him? (See Schürer, Jewish People, Div. 1, Vol. II, pp. 17-37.) 4. How much of a knowledge of Jesus may we presuppose on the part of the Nobleman? 5. What leads Jesus to say "Except ye see signs and wonders," etc. (43)? Do these words undervalue the miracles? 6. Give the tests of faith which Jesus puts upon the man. 7. Show that the cure is clearly preternatural. 8. Study the progress of faith in this scene. 9. Is this miracle to be identified with the healing of the Centurian's servant (Matt. 8:5-13, Luke 7:1-10)? (See Weiss on one side and Godet on Luke in loco on the other.)

II. Topic for Research. The Relation of faith to healing. Look through all the instances of healing in the Gospels and note what is said of faith. Mark also those in which Jesus can do nothing because of unbelief. Then discuss the question carefully. In view of certain present-day teachings the subject is of vital interest.

II.

JESUS AT THE FEAST.

A — THE MIRACLE AT THE BETHESDA POOL.

Introductory. In all discussions upon the chronology of the Lord's life, John 5 : 1 occupies a very important place. Is the feast here referred to Purim or the Passover? If Purim, then the Ministry of Jesus was but two years long; if the Passover, then it was over three years in length.

*For Literature, etc., see Outlines I— III.

The subject is fully discussed in Andrews' Life of Our Lord and in Godet on John ; Andrews for the Passover, Godet for Purim. See also Gilbert's Student's Life of Jesus, Chapter VI, and Wieseler's Synopsis of the Four Gospels, pp. 204-220. Go carefully over the discussion. Whether the feast was the Passover or the Purim, we are of the opinion that the scenes at this feast closed the early Judean Ministry, a ministry crowded full of Messianic revelations but with comparatively small results. This fifth chapter is significant for John, not only because of the miracle, but more especially on account of the words of Jesus. They are rich in Messianic claims. The chapter also marks the beginning of the conflict throughout which "unfaith" develops, and the Messiahship of Jesus stands out in teachings which are unique and exalted. For convenience in study we can make no simpler, clearer division than that given by Laidlaw who divides the narrative into three scenes : At the Pool ; On the Street ; In the Temple.

AT THE POOL (2-9).

A man who has been a helpless invalid for nearly forty years is "made whole."

III. Suggestions and Questions for Study. 1. Where was the Pool of Bethesda ? (See Stewart's The Land of Israel, p. 181, and further references there cited.) 2. Why were the sick gathered about this pool ? Give the physical explanation of the current belief about the Angel. 3. You will note that the Revised Version has omitted verse 4. By what right ? (See Scrivener's Introduction to the Criticism of the N. T., Vol. II, p. 361 ; Westcott and Hort's Greek Test. (Harper's Edition), Vol. II, p. 77.) 4. Give the more correct translation of the word rendered "bed" in verses 8 and 9. 5. What right has Weiss to say that this man's infirmity was the result of a life of sin ?

IV. Topic for Research. The Sabbath according to the Pharisees. (See Edersheim's Life and Times of Jesus the Messiah, Vol. II, pp. 53-61 and appendix XVII, Vol. II, p. 777 ; Schürer, The Jewish People in the Time of Jesus Christ, Div. II, Vol. II, pp. 96-105 ; Hastings' B. D. article, Sabbath, Vol. IV, p. 320.)

ON THE STREET (10-13).

The happy man on his way to the Temple fastens upon himself the critical gaze of the Pharisees, since, forsooth, he is carrying his "mat" under his arm.

V. Suggestions and Questions for Study. 1. Do you think that Jesus acted in order deliberately to bring up the Sabbath-question? Give reasons for your answer. 2. What is peculiarly Pharisaic in the attitude here depicted? 3. In what respect does the man's obedience thoroughly commend itself? 4. Give some of the elements of bigotry as illustrated in this street-scene.

IN THE TEMPLE (14-16).

Jesus seems to have sought the man and finding him in the Temple warned him. The man goes to the Jews and they turn upon Jesus.

VI. Suggestions and Questions for Study. 1. Why does Jesus seek the man whom He had cured? 2. "Sin no more" should be "continue no longer in sin." What light does this throw upon the case ? 3. What possible motive led the man to go straight to the Jews who, as he must have known, were hostile to Jesus? 4. Again in verse 16 we have an imperfect (in Greek) of repeated action to be translated in this way : Because he was doing (or was accustomed to do) these things on the Sabbath. This was not the first act of Sabbath-breaking. It is interesting to note in the Gospels the quiet, but firm disregard of the "traditions" which Jesus manifested whenever these traditions obscured or contravened some essential Spiritual principle.

VII. Topic for Research. Does the N. T. give any seconding to the teaching that all suffering has direct connection with personal sin? (See John 9 : 3, Luke 13 : 2, Acts 28 : 4, Matt. 9 : 2.)

B — THE TEACHINGS FOLLOWING THE MIRACLE.

There are two possible views of the words given in this chapter in verses 17-47. 1. They may be considered as a single address of Jesus based upon the miracle which He had just performed. 2. They may be looked upon as the substance of several addresses upon the Sabbath question, fused together in the mind and memory of the Apostle and connected with this typical instance of the cure at Bethesda. As the first view is the one usually taken in the commentaries, it is necessary to give some reasons only for the second. These are : (*a*) The statement in verse 15, "because He was doing these things on the Sabbath," *i. e.*, "because He was accustomed to do these things on the Sabbath." The address fits this broader statement. According to verse 10, it is the carrying of the bed that stands out as unlawful. The reply of Jesus touches a larger violation than this. (*b*) Except for the introductory scene, which is certainly typical of others, the discourse is without historical setting. It ends, as has been said of it, "in the air," *i. e.*, we know nothing of its effect. (*c*) Its intricacy of thought. A notable example of this is in verses 19-22. This is a mark of Johannine form. Indeed, this address, if considered from the second view-point, gives opportunity for studying this very Johannine form. The question may then be justly asked, how do we know that we have the substance of the words of Jesus. Two reasons may be given in reply. (1) The character of the utterances. They are not after the fashion of human imagination. (2) The support given to their genuineness by like statements of Jesus in the Synoptics. To see this, compare verses 17, 18 with Mark 2 : 27, 28 ; 19, 20 with Matt. 11 : 27 (a passage rising to the height of Johannine Christology) ; 21-24 with Matt. 11 : 27 ; 28 : 18 ; 10 : 40 ; 25-29 with Matt. 25 : 46 ; 30 with Matt. 26 : 39 ; 37-40 with Luke 24 : 26, 27, 44-46 ; 41-44 with Matt. 13 : 15 ; 18 : 1-4 ; 45-47 with Luke 16 : 29-31. The whole discourse divides itself into two parts, 17-30, 31-47. Let us take each in order.

VIII. Analysis of Verses 17-30.

> *Theme.* The Absolute and Constant Fidelity of the Son's Working to the Father's, 17.
>
> 1. The Son does nothing of his own initiative, 19.
> 2. The Son does whatever the Father does, 19b, (and this is possible) since
>
>   (*a*) The Father shows to the Son all the things which He (the Father) doeth, 20a.
>
>   (*b*) The Father will include in His showing greater works than have as yet been shown, 20b, *e. g.*
>
> Quickening (21) { Spiritual Resurrection, 24a, c, 25. { Bodily Resurrection, 28, 29a.
>
> Judgment (22) { Spiritual Judgment, 24b. { Final Judgment, 29 b.
>
> The purpose of *a* and *b* (verse 23).

It is with such exalted claims as these that Jesus defends His right to work miracles of healing on the Sabbath.

IX. Questions and Suggestions for Study. 1. In what sense does "the Father work until now"? Compare the statement with Gen. 2 : 2, 3. 2. In what two ways does Jesus in this Gospel oftenest speak of Father? (See concordance.) 3. How does the expression "My Father" argue equality as the Jews assert? 4. Does "of Himself" refer to physical ability or moral attitude? 5. How do you interpret the word "seeth" in verse 19? 6. Do these statements impress you as of necessity originating with Jesus? Establish your answer. 7. What is the exact force of "whom He will" in verse 21? 8. Make a paraphrase of verses 19-23, *i. e.* express the relations of the thought in your own words. 9. Does verse 23 carry with it the implication of deity for the Son? 10. In what sense is it true that one "cometh not into judgment" (24)? 11. Interpret verse 26. 12. Compare verse 27 with 3:17, and explain the apparent contradiction. 13. What has the reason "because He is the Son of man" to do with what goes just before it? 14. Do verses 28 and 29 teach an universal resurrection? 15. What is meant by the phrase "resurrection of judgment" (29)? 16. Mark how verse 30 is a sort of summary of what goes before and an introduction to what comes after. 17. Write out all the Messianic claims found in this address. 18. This discourse is a notable revelation of the "Son-heart" of Jesus and Godet, who calls attention to this, well adds that not metaphysic but religious devotion opens the straightest way to its understanding.

X. Topic for Research. The Doctrine of the Union of the Son with the Father. See Stevens' Johannine Theology, pp. 102-126; Wendt, The Teaching of Jesus, Vol. II, pp. 151-178; Bruce, The Kingdom of God, pp. 178-186; Weiss, N. T. Theology, Vol. II, pp. 325-331.

XI. Analysis of 31-47.

THE WITNESS TO THE SON

I. In itself is complete and clear.

    since (a) It is not a mere self-witness but is that of another whose witness is true, 31, 32.

        (b) It is not from man, 34, even though the testimony of John the Baptist was valid and the Jews welcomed him for a season, 33a, 35;

        but

    since (a) It is in the works which the Father gave for accomplishment, 36.

        (b) It is in the Father's own declaration, 37.

        (c) It is in the Scriptures, 38-40.

II. To the Jews is inadequate and futile.

    since (a) They rejected the signs.

        (b) They had neither ear nor eye for the personal revelations of the Father, 37.

        (c) They were guilty of a blind bibliolatry, 38-40.

    The causes of a, b, c, are

        (a) In their lack of the love of God in their hearts (shown in the fact of verse 43).

        (b) In their purely selfish desires, 44.

    The perilous issue of a, b, c — Even Moses whom they trusted would condemn them, 45; the reason for this, 46.

XII. Suggestions and Questions for Study. 1. Fill in imaginatively the gap between 30 and 31, i. e. account for the change of theme. 2. What was the Jewish law about witnesses for establishing the truth of a statement? 3. Does the reference to John amount to a disparagement of the Baptist? 4. What is the meaning of "howbeit I say these things that ye may be saved"? 5. Note that Jesus says He *was* the lamp, etc. Why? 6. Does "ye were willing to rejoice," etc., throw light upon a temporary attitude of the rulers? Explain this. 7. What is the apologetic value of miracles? Are they included in the "works"? 8. In verse 37 it reads "He hath borne" witness. Note the varying interpretations of this. 9. What is bibliolatry? Is it possible in our day? 10. Give some instances of the way in which the O. T. Scriptures bear witness of Christ? 11. In what relation does verse 43 stand to 42? 12. Why does receiving glory from one another make faith impossible (44)? 13. Give some instances where Moses wrote of Christ.

XIII. Topics for Research. 1. Messianic Prophecy in the Pentateuch. 2. The meaning and use of the word "glory" in the N. T. (See Cremer's Biblico-Theological Lexicon.)

Outline Studies in the Gospel of John,

BY

JAMES STEVENSON RIGGS, D. D.,

Professor of Biblical Criticism in Auburn Theological Seminary, Auburn, N. Y.

Prepared for the Rhode Island Committee of Pastors.

*Outline Study VI.

CHAPTER VI.

THE CRISIS IN GALILEE.

If your study of chronology in connection with John 5:1, has led you to the conclusion that the feast there mentioned is Purim, then the events of this chapter took place about one month later. If you have decided for the Passover, then one whole year intervenes between chapters 5 and 6. Whichever scheme is followed, this event of the feeding of the five thousand with its subsequent teaching, brings us to the critical point of all that ministry of preaching and healing which is marked as Galilean. Again, it is true that it is not so much the miracle alone as what is said and done in consequence of the miraculous action of Jesus that interests John. The character of the true Messiah is, in this chapter, made to stand out not only against the disappointed misconceptions of the people, but in His vital relations to men. In chapter V, Jesus is presented to us as in intimate union with the Father and as the *source* of life. Now we are to see how in vital contact with men He may be the *support* of life. Indeed, in successive chapters John asks us to see the Messiah as the source of Life, Light and Love. There is no higher revelation of the Divine than this. The study of this chapter, therefore, is the study of another series of Messianic claims. The whole chapter may be divided into three parts: *A*—The narration of the miracles, 1-21. *B*—The discourses, 22-59. *C*—The Crisis, 60-71.

A 1—THE FEEDING OF THE FIVE THOUSAND. (1-14.)

1. **Suggestions and Questions for Study.** 1. In order to see how this event is placed, get clearly before yourself, in outline, all that is recorded as having taken place in Galilee—the teaching of the multitude, the training of the disciples, the events giving Jesus wide-spread fame, etc. (See Stevens and Burton's Harmony.) 2. Compare critically this account with that in the Synoptics and add, in their proper place, the details which Matthew, Mark and Luke respectively give. It is worth your while to try to construct carefully a full picture from the four narratives. 3. Why does John add "which is the Sea of Tiberias"? Give the history and general influence of Tiberias upon Galilee. (See G. A. Smith, Hist. Geog., p. 447ff.; B. D., Tiberias.) 4. Is the "great multitude" of verse 2 the same as that of verse 5?" 5. Where was "the mountain" of verse 3? 6. How do you explain the allusion to the Passover in verse 4? 7. With what statement does the "therefore" of verse 5 make connection? 8. Give as many reasons as you can for the working of the miracle. 9. In what sense did Jesus "try" Philip (6)? 10. How much is two hundred pennyworth? 11. Where was the place where the miracle was performed? 12. What reasons can you give showing that this was the greatest of the nature-miracles? 13. After thoughtful inspection mark those details in the narrative which seem to indicate an eye-witness. 14. What is the adequate reply to be given to all those who assert that we have in this scene no real miracle but simply a quickening of the spirit of generosity, so that the people shared their supplies with others? 15. In verses 14 and 15 we have a decisive proof of the historical character of this gospel, for these verses reflect accurately the current Messianic idea. (See Sibylline Oracles, III, 652-794; Psalms of Solomon (XVII, XVIII); Ethiopic Enoch, Chapters XXXVII-LXX. See, also, Goodspeed's Israel's Messianic Hope, Chapters IX, X.)

*For Literature, etc., see Outlines I-III.

II. Topic for Research. 1. Were there two miracles of feeding the multitude (see Matt. 15:32-38; Mark 8:1-9), or only one? (See Weiss, Life of Christ, Vol. II, 376ff.; Trench, Notes on the Miracles, p. 280ff., and commentaries in connection with each miracle.) 2. Were there two Bethsaidas? (See John 1:44; 12:21; also Josephus, Ant. XVIII, 2, 1; Smith, Hist. Geog., pp. 457, 458; B. D., Bethsaida.) The study of this question carries with it a careful examination of the geographical movements in connection with the events narrated. (See McGregor's Rob Roy on the Jordan, pp. 374-386.)

A 2—THE MIRACLE OF WALKING ON THE WATER. (16-21.)

III. Suggestions and Questions for Study. 1. Estimate the seriousness of the position of Jesus when the crowd came to take Him by force. 2. John says " He withdrew into the mountain "; what else did He do? (See Synoptics.) 3. Why was it imperative that the disciples should go away? 4. It is said (17) that " Jesus had not yet come to them." Were they expecting Him? Certainly not upon the water. Where then? 5. Give some account of the shores of Galilee, showing why quick and violent disturbances of the lake surface were easily possible. (See Smith, Hist. Geog., p. 444.) 6. From your study of the second of the topics of research give the possible positions of the boat, as described in verse 19. 7. What evidence have you from the accounts that Jesus walked upon the water and not upon the shore? 8. Does the "and immediately" (21) indicate a second miracle? Consider this critically. 9. Note and account for the variations in the accounts of the Synoptics. 10. What is it in this scene which makes appeal to John?

IV. Topic for Research. The Sea of Galilee. Get the picture of its physical appearance in the time of Jesus before your eye. Note its cities, its teeming population, the roads that led to it, its industries and the complex influences surrounding it. (Read Smith, Hist. Geog., Chapter XXI; Merrill, Galilee in the time of Christ, Sections VI-X; and, if possible, see literature cited by these authors.)

B—THE TEACHING OF JESUS. (22-59.)

Introductory. The events intermediate between the landing of the boat and the action of the people on the following day are found in the Synoptics. While doubtless many went away after the words of Jesus, many also passed the night near the scene of the miracle waiting for Jesus to come back from His mountain retirement. Meanwhile he had, unobserved, gone to the disciples and in the early morning was on the plain Gennesaret. The dawn of day revealed only a small boat upon the Eastern shore. The crowd soon discovered that Jesus was not on their side of the lake and, using some boats which had arrived from Tiberias as well as the ford across the Jordan (about two miles north of the lake), all hurried to Capernaum to find Him. They were doubtless yet intent upon their politico-religious schemes. We are not told just where they found Him, but their question "when camest Thou hither?" leads Jesus to speak. Before entering upon the study of the discourse itself, several features of it are worthy of careful consideration. (1) It moves forward in the form of dialogue. It is, however, the character of this dialogue that is remarkable. Like nearly all the dialogues in John, it is busy with the contrast between the true ideal sense and the false literal sense. One of John's favorite words is "true" in the sense of ideal. These dialogues seem to have in this respect a common pattern. (See 3:3-6; 4:9-15; 7:14-18; 8:21-24; 8:31-35, 53-58 and elsewhere.) (2) The repeated statements which are almost like fixed refrains, in 39, 40, 44, 54; see also 33, 50, 58; see also 35, 48, 51; also 54, 56, 59. Notice how the thought comes back to the same point. (3) The points where the connection is difficult to trace. (See verses 37, 43 and 46.) Connection in the discourses in the Synoptics is much more evident. The question which arises in connection with such considerations as these is, have we here, in view of them, the impress of the Evangelist? Keep this entirely distinct from the question "Have we the truth?" The truth is evidenced by the substance of what is said. The object in calling your attention to these features is to guide you in studying the *subjectivity* of John's Gospel. As in the previous chapter the discourse is based upon the miracle and the attitude of the people regarding it. The mixed audience was made up of those who were with Him " on the other side of the sea," those who had followed Him from the plain of Gennesaret and of the Scribes and Pharisees. If all that is given in 26-58 be looked upon as one discourse, it may be divided as follows: Part I, 26-40; II, 41-51; III, 52-58. In these divisions are two parentheses, 37-40 and 43-46. Godet treats these parts as separate discourses; so does Westcott, and suggests for each a change of scene and audience. Only the last discourse is given, according to Westcott, in the Synagogue in Capernaum. We have, then, a grouping of the discourses with reference to the miracle of the bread. The same features (1, 2, 3, given above) merit attention even if you conclude for a group of discourses. Let us take each part in order.

U. Analysis of Part I. (26-40.) THE TRUE BREAD.
    I. Its Source.
        (*a*) It is given by the Father, 32, through the Son, 27.
        (*b*) It comes down from Heaven, 32, 33.
    II. Its Nature.
        (*a*) It is personal and vital and spiritual, 33, 35.
    III. Its Power.
        (*a*) It gives life, 33.
        (*b*) It satisfies hunger forever.
    IV. Its Attainability.
        It is gained not by physical exertion, 27, but by spiritual work, 27, which work is believing in Jesus Christ, 29, or coming to Him in faith. This last thought of "coming" suggests the attitude of the Jews and the truth given in 37-40 which may be analyzed as follows:
           (1) The certainty of the realization of the coming in the case of those whom the Father is giving, 37a. They shall reach Him (the Son).
           (2) The surety of the issue to those who come, 37b.
        Reasons for (1) and (2).
        (*a*) Jesus came to do the Father's will.
        (*b*) That will includes (1) and (2)
          Viewed from the divine side, } both of these
          Viewed from the human side, }
          Involving { (*a*) Present salvation,
                   { (*b*) Future resurrection.

UI. Suggestions and Questions for Study. 1. Give the exact bearing of the answer of Jesus (26) upon the question asked Him. 2. Explain the difference between the Typical and the Symbolic use of a miracle. Which have we here? 3. What is the exact equivalent of "*meat*" which "abideth unto eternal life" in spiritual things? 4. What do you think of the suggestion that "sealed" in verse 27 refers to the custom of bakers who stamped their bread with their own names? 5. Can you explain how "believing" is to be conceived as a work? Note also that Jesus uses the singular "work," while His questioners speak of "works." 6. Jesus says "believe *in* Him whom He hath sent"; His hearers, "believe Him" (30). What is the difference? 7. What was the Jewish tradition regarding Manna? (See Westcott in loco.) 8. Give the double contrast in verse 32. 9. What important advance in His teaching does Jesus make in verse 35? 10. The questioners asked Jesus what sign He had to show. Where does He meet that requirement? 11. Do you find in verses 37 and 39 the doctrine of election? (See Godet and Reynolds in loco.) If you are a student of the Greek, it will pay you to examine the Greek closely in this section. 12. In the phrase "eternal life" is "eternal" primarily qualitative or quantitative? 13. Does the phrase "at the last day" argue for or against a conception of resurrection as a process in John's thought? 14. Write out the Messianic claims in this section.

UII. Analysis of Part II. (41-51.) COMING TO (*i. e.* believing in) THE SON.
    I. The inner divine working necessary to it—the drawing of the Father, 44, which is through "teaching" and "learning," 45, but not by direct vision; only the Son has this, 46.
    II. The blessing which it secures—eternal life, 47, since the Son is the bread of life, 48, which bread does not, as did the Manna, leave men to die, 49, but which, because it is the living bread from Heaven, 51, gives eternal life. That bread is His flesh, 51.

VIII. Suggestions and Questions for Study. 1. Mark the literal understanding over against the ideal teaching in 41, 42. 2. Note the words "whose father and mother we know." How often is the miraculous conception of Jesus referred to in the Gospels? 3. Several questions arise in connection with verse 44 : (a) Does "draw" give basis for the doctrine of "irresistible grace"? (b) Does the Father "draw" only certain ones from among men? (c) How is the "drawing" further explained? (d) Is the initiative in the whole activity of redemption always taken by God? 4. Note Godet's comment : "Between these extreme terms 'draw' and 'raise up' lies the whole development of spirititual life." 5. Does the section teach the preëxistence of the Son? 6. What is the connection between verses 48 and 47? 7. Show that verse 51 is not a mere repetition of verse 50. 8. How often is the thought of the Incarnation emphasized in this section? 9. Mark any Messianic claims.

IX. Analysis of Part III. (52-58.) THE APPROPRIATION OF LIFE.

    I. The means to it—eating the flesh of the Son of Man and drinking His blood, 53.

    II. The resulting blessings.

        (a) Possession of eternal life, 54, 57, 58.

        (b) Bodily resurrection at the last day, 54.

        (c) Abiding of the believer in the Son.

        (d) The indwelling of the Son in the believer.

X. Suggestions and Questions for Study. No part of this discourse requires more careful reflective study than this. It is beset with questions of wide import. The two following demand earnest consideration : (1) Do "flesh and blood" mark simply the entire nature of the Son or are they to be separated in thought and "the blood" associated with the sacrificial, atoning death of Christ? In other words have we here a Johannine expression of Pauline doctrine? (See Godet on one side and Reynolds on the other.) (2) It is well known that John omits the account of the institution of the Eucharist. Are these words spoken with that solemn sacrament in view? Are they sacramental requirements before the time of the sacrament? The fatal Passover is yet one year distant. Does Jesus anticipate it here? In addition to these two questions which ought to have full discussion, the following need attention : (1) Was this symbolism of "eating and drinking" entirely strange to the Jews? (See Reynolds in loco.) (2) Why should "Son of Man" be used in this connection? (3) What does "abiding in Him" mean? (4) How does a man know that Christ dwells in him? (5) Paraphrase verse 57 so as to bring out its full meaning.

XI. Topic for Research. The conception of faith in John. The word faith is not found in the Fourth Gospel. One must, therefore, study the conception through the verb "to believe." Gather all the passages with the use of a concordance, classify them, and get conclusions inductively. (See also Wendt, Teaching of Jesus, Vol. II, 329-339 ; Weiss, Bib. Theol. of N. T., Vol. II, 363-370 ; Stevens, Johannine Theol., Chapter IX.)

C—THE CRISIS—(60-71.)

XII. Suggestions and Questions for Study. 1. What was the "hard saying" referred to in 60 ? 2. In verse 62 Jesus alludes to His Ascension. Show how this reference bears on the succeeding verse (63). Was the Ascension necessary to make Christianity vital? Show how. 3. What beginning is referred to in "from the beginning" (64)? 4. Discuss briefly the problem here set forth regarding Judas. 5. Make clear the connection between 64 and 65 by a paraphrase. 6. Do you think that old Messianic hopes were still active in those who "went back?" 7. Do the words of Peter mark an advance upon the conceptions of that day when he found the Messiah (1:41)? In regard to the chapter as a whole, the following judgment is true. "It shows a great superiority over the Synoptics in the sense and appreciation it reveals of the true situation, as a crisis in the development and definition of the Messianic character. The Johannine narrative, "dove-tailed" into the Synoptic, makes the latter much more intelligible."

Outline Studies in the Gospel of John,

BY

JAMES STEVENSON RIGGS, D. D.,

Professor of Biblical Criticism in Auburn Theological Seminary, Auburn, N. Y.

Prepared for the Rhode Island Committee of Pastors.

*Outline Study VII.

CHAPTER VII.

ı   JESUS AT THE FEAST OF TABERNACLES.

Between the occurrence of the events narrated in Chapter VI and those in Chapter VII intervenes a space of at least six months, for the Feast of Tabernacles was celebrated in October. Jesus had made in this intervening time journeys toward Tyre and Sidon, into the Decapolis and into Northern Galilee where the Transfiguration took place. With the Crisis in Galilee, however, John's interest in the ministry in the northern province came to an end. The scene is immediately shifted to Jerusalem. We are introduced into the thick of conflicting estimates and again made to see the Messiah in the claims which are set over against these estimates. The whole chapter is full of action. The scene is crowded with all sorts and conditions of men—"Jews," the multitude, the people of Jerusalem, the Sadducees, the Pharisees and disciples. Here "the crisis becomes hotter, the divisions, the doubts, the hopes, the jealousies and the curiosity of the Jews are vividly portrayed. We see the mass of the populace, especially those who had come up from Galilee, swaying to and fro, hardly knowing which way to turn, inclined to believe but held back by the more sophisticated citizens of the metropolis. In the background looms the dark shadow of the hierarchy itself entrenched behind its prejudices and refusing to hear the cause that it has already prejudged. A single timid voice is raised against this injustice, but is at once fiercely silenced." Over against all this stands the calm, serene, majestic figure of the Messiah. The chapter presents several features which are worthy of careful attention. (1). A fulness of details which argues for an eye-witness. (2) Illustrations of the thematic character of John's presentation of Christ's teaching. (3) A portrayal of the nature and strength of the antagonism whose issue was Calvary. For convenience of study, the chapter may be divided into three parts.. 1. The conversation of Jesus in Galilee with His brethren, 1-13. 2. His appearance at the Feast and His words at various junctures, 14-39. 3. The results of his teaching, 40-53.

*For Literature, etc., see Outlines I-III.

DIVISION A — (1-13). The Conversation in Galilee with His Brethren.

T. Suggestions and Questions for Study. 1. When did the Jews first plan to kill Jesus? 2. Give some of the results of the "Walk" in Galilee. 3. Give a full account of the Feast of the Tabernacles—its purpose, ritual and general character. (See Edersheim: The Temple and its Services, Chapter XIV; Hastings' B. D., Vol. 1, p. 861.) 4. What do His brethren mean in saying "that Thy disciples also may behold Thy works" (3)? 5. Show in what points the whole situation here is similar to that at Cana, John 2:3-9. 6. Interpret verse 6. 7. Is the word "hate" to be taken in its full sense? Why "cannot"? 8. Are Jesus' words in verse 8 inconsistent with His action in verse 10? 9. How would He go up "publicly" to the Feast? 10. Why were the Jews so eager to find Jesus at the Feast? Answer this quite fully. 11. Mark the influence of the "Jews" upon the people. How do you account for it, seeing that the Sadducees on the one side taught a completely heterodox theology while the Pharisees on the other laid upon them the heavy burden of the traditions?

TT. Topic for Research. The general character of the people of Galilee. (See Merrill, Galilee in the Time of Christ, Sections XII-XIV; Schürer, Div. II, Vol. I, pp. 1-56; Hastings' B. D., "Galilean"; Smith's Hist. Geog., pp. 421-425, and instances from Josephus there cited.)

DIVISION B, including four Discourses (14-39).

TTT. The First Discourse—(16-24). *Theme:* HIS TEACHING.

1. Whose it really is (16).
2. How its heavenly origin may be tested.
    (a) Confirmation of the principle of verse 17, (18).
    (b) Application of this principle or test to the Jews, 19, 22-24. Had they kept the *spirit* of the Mosaic law, they would not have condemned Him. Their judgment which was according to appearance had not only led to conspicuous inconsistency but had revealed that seeking of their own glory which made them incompetent to estimate rightly His teaching.

TU. Suggestions and Questions for Study. 1. Note that we have nothing given us of the teaching of that day referred to in verse 14. 2. Give some account of education in Palestine in the time of Jesus. (See Hastings' B. D., "Education", Vol. I, p. 649; Edersheim, Sketches of Jewish Social Life, Chapters VII, VIII; Schürer, Div. II, Vol. II, p. 44 ff., School and Synagogue; also Div. II, Vol. I, p. 306 ff., Scribism.) 3. To what do the questioners refer in the word "letters" (15)? 4. It is needful to make a careful exegetical study of the principle unfolded in verse 17. (See Luthardt and Godet in loco.) 5. Put into syllogistic form the argument of verse 18. 6. Do you think the expression "Thou hast a devil" is the equivalent of our saying "You are crazy"? If so, does this throw any light upon the whole subject of demonic possession? 7. To what does Jesus refer in the "one work" of verse 21? Remember, if you have made John 5:1 a passover, that you are at least eighteen months away from that passover. 8. Give in brief the history of circumcision. Was it practised by any other peoples than the Jews? 9. What is the real point that Jesus is making in this whole reference to circumcision? 10. Paraphrase verse 24 so as to bring out its full force and bearing.

V. Topic for Research. Should verses 15-24 be removed from this chapter and placed immediately after 5 :47? In seeking to answer this question consider carefully (*a*) the suitability of the connection if the verses are tranferred to the Fifth chapter, (*b*) the connection of the thought in Chapter 7 after they have been removed. The subject of "displacements" in John's Gospel has in recent years been much discussed. It calls for careful exegetical work and critical discussion of the connections of thought. The following order of materials in this part of the gospel is suggested as giving most clearly the proper development of John's plan: Chapter 4; 6:1-51; 5:1-47; 7:15-24; 7:1-13, 25-36, 45-52, 37-44. Examine this carefully. (See also Wendt, The Gospel according to John, pp. 85-96; Biblical World, Jan. 1899; Fisher, Grounds of Theistic and Christian Belief, new edition of 1902, p. 266 ff.; Studien und Kritiken, 1893, Heft 2.)

VI. The Second Discourse—(25-32). *Theme:* HIS ORIGIN.

1. The people claim to know it and therefore conclude against His Messiahship, 27.
2. Jesus declares that it is really unknown by them, since they did not know God who sent Him, 28.
   (*a*) The basis of His knowledge of God, 29.
   (*b*) The outcome of the declaration of this basis, 30-32.

VII. Suggestions and Questions for Study. 1. If you are a student of the Greek, you should look carefully at the *Greek* form of the questions of verses 25, 26. 2. The perplexity all through this gospel is very faithful to the traditional ideals of the Messiah. You should know these well in order to appreciate the accuracy of the chapter. It certainly is no second century production. 3. What is meant by "We know this man whence he is"? 4. It was one of the traditional teachings regarding the Messiah that he should come forth from concealment (verse 27). 5. Is the expression "you both know me and know whence I am" to be taken ironically or literally? Did Jesus use irony? 6. What is the sense of "know" in 28-29? 7. Give the interpretation of "true" in 28. Is preëxistence taught in verse 29? 8. Does verse 30 indicate miraculous restraint or is the restraint to be explained as the result of a providential arrangement of natural causes? If the latter, show it.

VIII. The Third Discourse—(33-36). *Theme:* HIS DESTINATION.

1. After a little while He shall go to it, 33.
2. It shall be neither discoverable nor attainable by the Jews, 34. The consequent perplexity of the Jews, 31, 36.

IX. Suggestions and Questions for Study. 1. Why "therefore" in verse 35? 2. What kind of seeking does Jesus refer to in 34? 3. What shall the "not finding" be really due to? 4. Is the "cannot" of the same verse to be "morally" interpreted? 5. Mark the contrast between the true ideal sense and the false literal sense in 35. 6. Do you think that their suppositional question is too crude to be genuine? (See Godet in loco.)

X. Topic for Research. The Sadducees, their origin, position, religious views, etc. (See Schürer, Jewish People in the time of Christ, Div. II, Vol. II, pp. 29-43; Hastings' B. D., IV, pp. 349-351, and the literature cited at the end of the article "Pharisees".)

XI. The Fourth Discourse (on the Last Day of the Feast) — (37-39). *Theme :* THE TRUE FOUNTAIN. To which every thirsty man should come, 37.
      (a) The blessed result of the coming, 38.
      (b) The real meaning of this result, 39.

XII. Suggestions and Questions for Study. 1. What were the significant features of the "eighth" day of the feast? 2. Do you think that the words of Jesus are suggested by the ritual in connection with the pool of Siloam? Look into this carefully. It will be of interest to acquaint yourself with the recent excavations of Dr. Bliss at the pool of Siloam. (See Bliss, Excavations at Jerusalem.) 3. Give the spiritual equivalent of "thirst". 4. Interpret "out of his belly shall flow rivers of living water." 5. Note the comment of the evangelist in 39. 6. Just what is meant by the words "the Spirit is not yet given"? Was not the Spirit active in all these instances mentioned in verse 31, "many believed on Him"? 7. How is the glorification of Jesus related to the giving of the Spirit? 8. Could not the Spirit come until Jesus was glorified? Why? In short, make clear to yourself the position and work of the Spirit before Pentecost. He certainly has always been existent and active.

DIVISION C—The Results of the Teaching (40-53).

1. Upon the Multitude. Their perplexity, 40-44.
2. Upon the Officials. The Meeting of the Sanhedrin and the Interposition of Nicodemus, 45-53.

XIII. Suggestions and Questions for Study. 1. Classify the hearers according to their attitudes. Has John seemingly a special purpose in introducing them with their various questions and perplexities? 2. Can you see any good reason for placing these verses 45-52 before the section, 37-44? 3. What was the authority of the Sanhedrin? 4. Just what had it commissioned the officers to do? 5. Does the question in 48 contain a common appeal for the validity of orthodoxy? 6. How did the learned of Judea in Christ's day regard the common people? (See Godet in loco.) 7. Do the Jews really answer the question of Nicodemus? 8. What is the purport and purpose of their question?

XIV. Topic for Research The Fourth Gospel and the Old Testament. Mark its reference to O. T. types, to O. T. prophecies and to any other features of the O. T. The study of this topic involves a careful reading of the Gospel in order to gather out all the O. T. allusions. Classify these, get their exegetical setting, and then think to conclusions. (See also Westcott, Introduction to Gospel, p. 66; Godet, Introduction to Gospel, Vol. I, p. 166.)

Outline Studies in the Gospel of John,

BY

JAMES STEVENSON RIGGS, D. D.,

Professor of Biblical Criticism in Auburn Theological Seminary, Auburn, N. Y.

Prepared for the Rhode Island Committee of Pastors.

---

*Outline Study VIII.

CHAPTER VIII.

THE RUPTURE IN JERUSALEM.

You will note that the first eleven verses of this chapter are bracketed. They contain a story, which, genuine though it may be, does not belong here. For a full discussion of its place, authority and value, see Harper's edition of Westcott and Hort's Greek Test., Vol. II, pp. 82-88; also the commentaries in loco. Reynolds gives a clear discussion of it; so does Godet. Our study begins with verse 12 and we have in this chapter a presentation of the Messiah in scenes and circumstances much like those in chapter seven. The exact time of these scenes cannot be stated. Jesus continued probably sometime in Jerusalem after the Feast of Tabernacles was over and the events here narrated are probably selected from many that occurred in those days. So, too, the teaching is in all liklihood a condensed Johannine rendering of the words of Jesus in which we find, now an actual deliverence of the Master, now, the substance of an address, now, an explanation of the evangelist. The chapter bristles with opposition to the claims of Jesus and is rich in the evidence of an eye-witness of the scenes it depicts. It gives the actual rupture of Jesus with the Jews. In studying, two or three considerations should be kept in mind: (*a*) that the discourses are made up largely of reminiscences of important emphatic statements, which came in the course of prolonged discussions. The evidence for this is in the quick change of theme and in the difficulty at times of getting the connection of thought (see 12-16); (*b*) that the accuracy for the reminiscences is vouched for in the result which they brought about. The crisis in Jerusalem came out of the same disappointment that had caused the crisis in Galilee. The teachings of this chapter show us how Jewish pride and expectation were rebuked and how all mere Jewish claims were reckoned insufficient. The true Messiah spoke and never did He seem more ideally true than when the evangelist saw Him confronting the confessedly best men of the nation with claims and conceptions which had in them no trace of earthly substance. For convenience of study, we may divide the whole into three parts: 12-20; 21-30; 31-59. Let us take them in order.

I. **Part I—**(12-20). **Analysis.**

Theme: CHRIST'S WITNESS—I AM THE LIGHT OF THE WORLD.

    I.   The Ground of this Witness, 14.
    II. Its Legality, 18.
    III. The Reason Why it is not Accepted, 19.

II. **Suggestions and Questions for Study.** 1. What was the occasion of the figure "the light of the world"? What is its significance? 2. What do you understand by "the light of life"? 3. Compare verse 12 with 1 John 1:1-7; also mark the parallel in the prologue. 4. What was the probable motive of the Pharisees in their objection (13)? 5. To this objection Jesus makes a double answer. Give its two parts. 6. Show how the reason given establishes the truthfulness or adequacy of the witness (14). 7. What is the connection of thought between verses 14, 15? 8. Is verse 16 a digression? Prove your answer. 9. Note the change of word in the Greek for the English word "true" in 16. 10. How does the reason "because I am not alone" establish an "ideal judgment"? (See

---

16.) 11. Can you give any clear explanation of the words "the father that sent me beareth witness of me"? Where would you look for the proof of this assertion? 12. What is the tone of the question "where is thy Father" (19)? 13. The negative particles and the conditional sentence in the Greek of verse 19 are worthy of attention. 14. State concisely what we know of the Father by knowing the Son. 15. Locate the treasury in the Temple. 16. What were just the circumstances which made evident the fact that "his hour was not yet come" and the consequent inadvisability of seizing Him? 17. Compare the whole statement about witnessing with 5 : 36-38 and 14 : 10, 11. Do they explain each other?

III. Topic for Research. THE CONSCIOUSNESS OF JESUS. Was it a human consciousness taught by the Spirit, or was it a consciousness of Himself as God with the attendant attributes of omniscience and omnipotence? This question is more significant than at first appears. It is suggested by such a statement in the text as "I know whence I came and whither I go". If you wish to work out an answer for yourself, it will be necessary to gather together from the gospel all such statements as given above and come to a conclusion regarding them. The question is really the critical question for Kenotic theories regarding Jesus. Help will be found in the following literature: Moorhouse, The Teaching of Christ; Mason, The Conditions of the Lord's Life on Earth; Gore, The Incarnation of the Son of God; Adamson, The Mind of Christ; Fairbairn, The Place of Christ in Modern Theology; Weiss, Life of Christ, Vol. I, 290-292, 322-336; Gore, Dissertations in Subjects Connected with the Incarnation, pp. 71-225; Beyschlag, N. T. Theology, Vol. I, 73-75, 236-266.

IV. Part II—(21-30). Analysis.

While studying this section it may be well to bear in mind the comment of Sanday: "The connection appears to be confused by that reiterated self-assertion, which was, indeed, there but which the evangelist regards somewhat too exclusively. We can well believe that there was more in the original of the winning pathos of the lament over Jerusalem (Luke 19 : 42-44); in which case we could perhaps better understand the concluding statement, "As He spake these words many believed on Him." See if your study of the passage leads you to agree with this judgment.

Theme: THE SERIOUSNESS OF THE DIFFERENCE BETWEEN THE
JEWS AND HIM.

1. In reference to their destiny—they cannot come to Him, 21; all their seeking after Him shall but issue in death in the midst of their sin, 21.

2. In reference to their innermost nature—they are "from beneath" while He is "from above", 21.

This difference can be entirely removed by faith; unless it be so removed, death in the midst of their sins is the issue, 24.

3. In reference to judgment—they are yet to be the subjects of many sentences of judgment, 26.

(a) These judgments are part of the message of Him who is true, 26.

(b) They must therefore be spoken, painful though they may be, 26.

Conclusion. The time is coming when you shall understand this radical difference between you and Me and also that My claims are true. Five distinct claims are asserted in 28, 29. *Note.* The compacted character of the thought makes analysis difficult. The above is meant to show the general relations of the statements made by the Master.

V. Suggestions and Questions for Study. 1. Explain the "seeking" to which Jesus refers. Get also the specific meaning of "sin" in verse 21. 2. What are the spiritual equivalents of the spatial relations, "go", "come", in 21, 22? How do you spiritually interpret the invitation (in spatial form) "come to Jesus"? 3. Note again the spatial descriptions "from beneath" "from above". Interpret the latter. 4. Is there any difference between "ye shall die in your *sin*", and "ye shall die in your *sins*"? 5. The revised version says "except ye believe that I am *He*" (24). The same form of expression occurs in verses 28 and 58. The Greek has no predicate after the verb. What is the full force of the statement? 6. Discuss fully the last clause of verse 25. (See commentaries in loco.) 7. Give the relation in thought of the clause "howbeit He that sent Me," etc., etc. (26), to what immediately precedes. 8. Note also in this chapter the frequent exhibitions of the literal interpretations of the Jews over against the spiritual, ideal presentations of Jesus. 9. Did the Crucifixion and the Resurrection bring the Jews to an understanding? 10. State the Messianic claims given in verses 28, 29.

VI. Topics for Research. THE DOCTRINE OF SIN IN JOHN'S GOSPEL. With a concordance get together all the statements made upon the subject. Through an inductive study come to conclusions. See also Beyschlag, N. T. Theology, Vol. I, pp. 228-230; Westcott, The Epistles of John, pp. 37-40; Stevens' Johannine Theology, Chapter VI.

VII. Part III—(31-59).

It will help to clearness to study this third part of the chapter in three subdivisions 31-36; 37-47; 48-59. Jesus is at first speaking to a mixed audience of believers and opponents. It is at verse 37 that the tone changes and the opposition becomes keener until the outbreak of verse 59. At verse 48 the discourse turns from the consideration of the Jews to Jesus Himself. The whole section in its appeal to descent from Abraham, in its bald literalisms, in its interpretations of demonic possession and in its fierce refusal of such claims as imply an assumption of the divine, gives evidence of an eye-witness. There is also a tone in this section which of itself makes us think of John, that son of thunder, who once wished to call down fire on an inhospitable Samaritan village and who, in the first epistle bearing his name, deals in short, sharp, straight-edged descriptions of character, position and destiny. Listen to these words, "Ye are of your father the devil, and the lusts of your father it is your will to do". "Because I say the truth ye believe me not". "Ye hear not, because ye are not of God". "If I should say I know Him not, I would be like unto you, a liar". It has been well said that in all this "there is none of that yearning pity that the attentive ear may distinguish as a deep sustained underchord beneath the most withering invectives of the Synoptics." The section also presents a clear picture of the inextinguishable national pride of the Jews.

First Subdivision—(31-36).

> *Theme:* ABIDING IN THE WORD.

1. Its significance—true discipleship, 31.
2. Its issue (a) Knowledge of the truth, 32.
   (b) True freedom, 32.
   The objection of the Jews, 33.
       The reply of Jesus to this objection; which may be given in the two following arrangements.
          1. The service of sin is slavery to sin.
             They were the servants of sin.
          ∴ They were in slavery.
          2. Sonship and slavery are opposed.
             Only the Son can make them sons.
          ∴ If the Son gave them freedom through Sonship, they would be free indeed.

Note. The thought in 34-36 is quite elliptical.

VIII. Suggestions and Questions for Study. 1. Note the clear distinction between "believed in Him" (30), and "believed Him" (31). It is to the latter that he addressed the word "abide". 2. What does "abide in the word" mean? 3. What "truth" is it that makes free? Can you show how? 4. How could the Jews say "we have been slaves to no one"? 5. Put the intermediate thoughts needful to make 35, 36 clear. 6. Are the "truth" and the "Son" practically identical as factors making one free?

Second Subdivision—(37-47).

> *Theme:* THE SPIRITUAL PARENTAGE OF THE JEWS.

1. It is not Abraham.
      since (a) Their doings are in line with another inspiration, 38.

(*b*) They seek to kill Him who speaks them to God's truth. Abraham would not do this, 40.

(*c*) They do the works of their father (the devil), 41.

2. It is not God.

since (*a*) They would, then, love Him for He came from God not of His own initiative but as sent, 42.

(*b*) They are the children of the devil, 44.

(*c*) They do not believe Him who speaks the truth, 45.

(*d*) They who are children of God give ear to the words of God, 47.

IX. Suggestions and Questions for Study. 1. Again mark the literal interpretation over against the ideal presentation of Jesus. 2. What is meant by "hath not free course to you" (37)? Does this reason give a hint as to the relation between "truth" and spiritual insight? 3. What do you understand by that direct vision of God given in "the things which I have seen with my Father" (38)? This "vision of God" is referred to also in 3:32 and 6:46. 4. Is "children" in verse 39 to be taken physically or spiritually? 5. Our English version renders two different Greek verbs by the same verb "speak". It is of value to note the different force of each. See especially verses 38, 40, 43, 44. 6. Give the underlying connection of thought between 40-41a and 41b-42. (See Westcott in loco.) 7. Give the exact bearing for the reason "for I came forth" etc., etc., and "for neither have I come" etc., etc., in verse 42. 8. Note the distinction between "speech" and "word" in 43. Consult the Greek. 9. Does verse 44 commit Jesus to the belief in a personal devil? 10. Compare verse 44 with 1 John 3:8-12. Does John get his truth from the words of Jesus, or do you think that John's strong feeling has given color and tone to the declarations of his Master? In other words is verse 44 a Johannine rendering? 11. Paraphrase "and stood not in the truth because there is no truth in him" (44), so as to bring out its full force. 12. What does "therefore" refer to, the liar or the lie? 13. Note the basal reason of all spiritual deafness "because ye are not of God" (47). See also 7:17; 18:37; 1 John 4:6. True sympathy opens the ear as well as the eye.

Third Subdivision—(48-59).

It is well to note that in this section we have presented to us a typical method of men whose argument has been refuted by unanswerable reasoning—the resort to personal abuse. It is the immediate precursor of violence as it marks the rapid rise of feeling. Passion dictates when reason is humiliated. Over against the charge that "He has a devil" and that He is a blasphemous egotist, Jesus calmly states His true purpose and position. These last words bring the open rupture. The changing themes do not enable one to gather all the teaching under a single subject.

X. Suggestions and Questions for Study. 1. Measure fully the insult in "thou art a Samaritan" (48). 2. Paraphrase verse 49 so as to bring out the force of the adversative in the Greek. 3. With what thought does verse 51 connect itself? Does "death" here mean physical death? How largely does John use the word with a spiritual meaning? (See concordance.) How would you prove from John that the spiritual meaning is not "annihilation"? 4. Mark again in 52, 53 the literalism over against the ideal spiritual meaning of Jesus. 5. In the Greek there is a distinction in the verbs translated "know" in verse 55. Can it be pressed? Mark also that the Greek has a perfect tense for one of the verbs. 6. Do you interpret verse 56 literally, or did Abraham see simply the *essentials* of Christ's day? 7. Do you consider verse 58 a direct unequivocal assertion of preëxistence? 8. If you do not supply a predicate, "Messiah", in verse 58, should it be supplied in 24 and 28? 9. What is in the answer of Jesus that is peculiarly offensive to the Jews? 10. Write out the Messianic claims of this chapter.

XI. Topic for Research. THE SINLESSNESS OF JESUS. This is an important subject in the thinking of our time. It will therefore repay careful study. We would suggest that the student make a careful analysis of Ullman's "The Sinlessness of Jesus".

Outline Studies in the Gospel of John,

BY

JAMES STEVENSON RIGGS, D. D.,

Professor of Biblical Criticism in Auburn Theological Seminary, Auburn, N. Y.

Prepared for the Rhode Island Committee of Pastors.

*Outline Study IX.

CHAPTERS IX AND X.

CHAPTER IX.

THE CURE OF THE MAN BORN BLIND.

The opening verse of this seems to connect it immediately with what goes before, in which case we would still be at Jerusalem just after the feast of Tabernacles. Chapters IX and X are, however, closely connected and from 10:22 Westcott argues that we must fix the time of the account which we are now to study about two months later when the feast of Dedication was observed. (See Godet for one view and Westcott for the other.) The Perean ministry has begun. Jesus has said farewell to Galilee. There are eight signs given us in John's gospel and this one of the cure of "the man born blind" is, in order, the sixth. It is the sign character of the incident which seems to have impressed it upon the mind of the evangelist. Blindness to the Jews was an especially pitiable limitation. Its darkness, helplessness and hopelessness made 'it significantly symbolic. Mark the great Messianic teaching of the chapter—"I am the light of the world." That is the central doctrine. All earnest discussion on the part of the neighbors, parents and Pharisees is in view of the miracle and the miracle reveals Him who is the light of the world. The chapter reserves careful study because of its *objective* character. It is made up almost entirely of shifting scenes full of action and the action is natural, vivid, and faithful both to times and circumstances. The words of Dr. Sanday are not too strong when he says, "If the opponents of miracles could produce a single Jewish document in which any event known not to have happened was described with so much minuteness and verisimilitude, then it would be easier to agree with them." It is well for the student to bear in mind that it is in this and in like chapters, *e. g.* 1:19-51, and VII that he must look critically for evidence of historic fidelity. Is the geography correct? Are the circumstances fitting? Are the mental and social phases in harmony with the times depicted? We are in this day well equipped with materials for giving answers to these questions, and the remarkable faithfulness with which the days from A. D. 27-30 are presented to us in the Fourth Gospel makes difficult the supposition of a writer who was not an eye-witness of the scenes he describes. One thing more is to be noted in our study of the chapter, and that is the development of faith on one

*For Literature, etc., see Outlines I-III.

side and unbelief on the other. The writer keeps these both in mind in nearly every part of the gospel. For convenience of study we divide the chapter into three parts: (1) The account of the miracle, 1-7; (2) the succeeding discussions and investigation, 8-34; (3) the spiritual outcome of the miracle, 35-41.

Part I. The Miracle—(1-7).

I. Suggestions and questions for Study. 1. What misconception lay at the basis of the question of the disciples (2)? 2. Give instances of judgments expressing a like misconception entertained by some people now. 3. There are four explanations offered of the connection between this man's blindness and sin: (*a*) Transmigration of souls, (*b*) pre-existence of souls, (*c*) a punishment of sins yet to be committed after he was born, (*d*) sins of the fathers visited upon the children. Of these (*c*) is not to be thought of and (*a*) and (*b*) were too exceptionally taught to be in the thought of the disciples. It is really not necessary to suppose that the disciples had any definite idea of the connection. 4. In what sense is the "purpose clause" in verse 3 to be taken? 5. What "works" are here referred to? 6. What do "day" and "night" signify in verse 4? 7. Interpret the statement "I am the light of the world." 8. Why does Jesus use the clay and the spittle? 9. Does He always use such means in the cure of blindness? (See Matt. 20:34.) 10. Why does He send him to the pool of Siloam? (See Godet in loco.) 11. If possible it would be well to acquaint one's self just at this point with the work done recently by Dr. Bliss at the ancient pool of Siloam. (See Excavations at Jerusalem 1894-1897, Chapters IV and V; see also the article Siloam in Hastings' B. D., IV, pp. 515, 516.) 12. Has John any special object in interpreting the name Siloam?

II. Topic for Research. 1. Give all the references in the Fourth Gospel to places in and about Jerusalem. Make a map of the ancient city and as far as possible locate these places.

Part II. THE SUCCEEDING DISCUSSIONS AND INVESTIGATION—(8-34).

III. Suggestions and questions for Study. 1. Give as exact a statement as you can of the detail found in verses 8-12. 2. Which of the parties mentioned in verse 9 probably asked the questions of 10 and 12? 3. Why do they take him to the Pharisees? 4. Give the three stages by which the examination progresses and note the developments on each side. 5. It is well to note that we have the record of seven miracles wrought on the Sabbath (Matt. 12:9; Mark 1:21, 29; Luke 13:14; 14:1; John 5:10; 9:6, 7). 6. What is the real point of difficulty for the Pharisees? 7. What is the dilemma for the others? Give both horns of it. 8. How does the man himself explain the situation? 9. Who are the "they" of verse 17 who asked the question? 10. What turn do the Jews take when they are confronted by the confession of the man? 11. Set forth the predicament of the parents and their method of escape. 12. Verse 22 indicates an advanced stage of opposition to Jesus. It is an interesting study to trace the progress of this antagonism to the Master, but one must use the Synoptics also for the purpose. 13. Give some account of excommunication among the Jews. (See Hastings' B. D. under this head.) 14. Note the pronounced, decided utterances of verses 24, 28, 32, 34. They breathe the spirit of wilful perversion. 15. Compare verse 24 with 7:27. 16. Is "sinner" in the N. T. used simply to mark a man who commits sin? 17. What kind of a tone lies behind the words of the cured man, as given in verses 25-27? 18. It will interest a student of the Greek to notice the Perfect in verse 29. 19. Paraphrase verse 30 so as to bring out its full force. 20. Put the blind man's argument in 31-33 into syllogistic form. 21. How can you parallel it with a line of argument that can be used in our day, based also upon experience. (An interesting side-light will be found in the last chapter of a recent book: Coe's Religion of a Mature Mind.) 22. Note carefully how a clinching argument is met by personal abuse (34). There is fine scorn in the "teachest thou us" of verse 34. This short section gives opportunity for studying the spirit and attitude of that kind of narrow dogmatism which in the presence of unwelcome facts will try any course to maintain itself. It is Godet who says that this entire chapter shows to Modern Criticism, in its treatment of the Supernatural, its own portrait. Can you trace the resemblances?

IU. Topic for Research. THE SYNAGOGUE. Its place and importance in Judaism; its history, structure and form of service. (See B. D., Vol. IV, 636 ff; Schürer, The Jewish People in the Time of Christ, Div. II, Vol. II, 52-89.)

Part III. THE SPIRITUAL OUTCOME OF THE MIRACLE—(35-41).

U. Suggestions and questions for Study. 1. In order to get the significance of the question addressed by Jesus to the cured man (35) we must refer the student to the topic for research in Outline I, and the literature there given. "Son of Man" is more likely the true reading; not "Son of God." 2. Give the different meanings of "seeing" in verse 39; a paraphrase of the verse will show you whether you understand it. Compare also Luke 10:21; Matt. 11:25; Matt. 12:31-33. 3. It is well to note that the Greek form of the question in 40 requires the translation "We are not blind, too, are we?" They evidently expected Jesus to say "no." 4. Carefully study the answer of Jesus in 41. Just how is sin to be conceived of here? The terms used all through this brief conversation keep before us the symbolical character of the miracle.

CHAPTER X.

It is an unfortunate division which brings a chapter heading in between 9:41 and the thought of Chapter X. The very form of the first sentence "verily, verily," indicates that a close relationship is marked. We include it, therefore, in the same outline with Chapter IX. Several questions arise in connection with the chapter which need special attention. The same old inquiry as has met us again and again comes to the front, *viz:* regarding the character and the degree of the Johannine impress upon it. This meets us at the opening in regard to the *form* of the teaching. Have we here parable or allegory? If the latter, is it Johannine or does it originate with Jesus? It would be well for the student to look critically at the parables of Jesus and mark their variety; also to see whether the general substance of the thought of this allegory cannot be paralleled in the Synoptics. The other question which suggests itself in connection with the chapter as a whole is whether there is descernible in it a Pauline influence. The exact form in which this was operative may have been to quicken the mind of the apostle to the value of certain teachings which might otherwise have been passed by. We shall call attention to these as we go on. Jesus speaks all through the chapter with His opponents in mind. Antagonism to Him is now rapidly intensifying. We are introduced in verse 22 to the feast of Dedication, observed in December. There are marks all through the chapter, in what may be called the objective parts of it, of an eye-witness of its events *e. g.*, "and Jesus walked in the Temple, in Solomon's Porch" (23); "How long dost thou make us to doubt?" (24); and "and Jesus went away again beyond the Jordan into the place where John at first baptized" (40). It will help to clearness if we divide the whole account into two main divisions—1-21, 22-42; and then subdivide these as follows: Part I into 1-6, 7-10, 11-18, 19-21; Part II into 22-30, 31-39, 40-42.

Part I—(1-21).

SUB-DIVISION A—(1-6). THE REAL SHEPHERD.

(a) Enters the fold by the door (2), in distinction from the one who gets in by some other way, 1.
  (2) Calls his sheep by name and leads them out, 3.
  (3) Is followed by his sheep because they know his voice, 4.

VI. Suggestions and questions for Study. 1. You will note that each mark of the real sheperd is set over against the opposite. Keep the preceding chapter in mind while interpreting. 2. An instructive, illuminating chapter on shepherd life will be found in Tristram's Eastern Customs in Bible Lands, VI; see also Hastings' B. D., Shepherd. 3. It is questionable how far each part of the figure should be pressed in the interpretation of this section; it would be better to get the broad teachings rather than attempt refinements of application. What are the broad teachings? 4. Does Jesus in the passage refer to a "Spiritual Israel"? 5. Is the idea of "knowing" as applied to Christians and illustrated in the perception of the sheep, peculiar to John? (See 1 John 2:13, 14; 3:3, 6; 4:6.)

SUB-DIVISION B—(7-10). THE DOOR.

VII. Suggestions and questions for Study. 1. Note the abrupt change of theme. Perhaps the word "door" had caught the attention of the hearers of the words just spoken, or this may be a short reminiscence of an address given at another time. 2. It is Tholuck who says that verse 8 seems to him one of the most difficult in the N. T. The words are difficult both in their connection and because of their inclusiveness, but their interpretation must be in connection with the immediate context. It is doubtful whether they refer to "false Messiahs" or to the "kings of former times." Note that the verb is in the present "*are* thieves and robbers." 3. Explain from your study of Pharisaism how it played the role of "thief and robber" as exhibited in verses 1 and 8. Just in what sense is Christ the "door" and translate into the spiritual equivalent "entering in." 4. Is the gift of life central to the mission of the Savior? 5. Life in its inner meaning cannot be defined, but can you make clear by yourself how the abundant life which Christ gives is made manifest. The simplicity of John's statements is sometimes our very hindrance to understanding them. This whole chapter merits earnest reflection and should have as far as possible translation into spiritual equivalents. 6. Do you think that Weiss has reason for saying that verses 7-10 are the words of the evangelist and not of Jesus?

VIII. Analysis. *Theme:* THE GOOD SHEPHERD.

Since:
    I. He is willing to give His life for the sheep (11, 15). In this He is the very opposite of the hireling, who flees when danger threatens the sheep, 12, 13.
        (*a*) The acts of sacrifice and resurrection were purely spontaneous on the part of Jesus, yet
    II. He knows His sheep and His sheep know Him, 14.
      The measure and character of this knowledge, 15.
    III. He will gather all His sheep into one flock, 16.
      Therefore the Father loves Him since for this purpose He takes His life again after laying it down that in the *resurrection* life He may "lead out" *all* the sheep, 17.
        (*a*) The acts of sacrifice and resurrection were purely spontaneous on the part of Jesus, yet (18 *a*, *b*)
        (*b*) They accorded with the will of the Father, 18 *c*.

IX. Suggestions and questions for Study. 1. Get the full significance of the word rendered "good" in our version. 2. A student of the Greek will be interested in the peculiar form "gives his life" (11). 3. It is well to note that all through this section the preposition translated "for" in "for the sheep" means "to the advantage of," not "in place of." 4. Verse 15 gives an excellent opportunity of looking into the Johannine word "know." 5. Does "other sheep I have" point to a universalism in the thought of the fold which is not true to Jesus' usual teaching? (See Matt. 8:11; Luke 13:28; Matt. 25:31; Matt. 28:19.) 6. Does the "therefore" of verse 17 point forward or backward? 7. What is the exact import of the resurrection of Jesus to His work of salvation? 8. How do you reconcile verse 18 with Acts 2:24? 9. Show the inner relation of 18 *c* with 18 *a*, *b*.

SUB-DIVISION D—(19-21). THE RESULT OF THESE TEACHINGS.

X. Suggestions and questions for Study. 1. Among whom did the division take place? 2. To what extent was demonic possession believed in among the Jews? (See Dr. Alexander's recent work on Demonic Possession, Chap. 2.) Note the significant word of interpretation "and is mad." 3. Was the conclusion of the second party (21) in accord with orthodox Jewish Theology?

XI. Topic for Research. THE FEAST OF DEDICATION. The history leading up to its institution. Its ritual and general character. (See B. D., Dedication; Edersheim, The Temple, its Ministry and Services, pp. 292, 293.)

Part II—(22-42).

In both of the sub-divisions of this part of the chapter we have short historical introductions to the addresses. It should be noted in passing how many of the addresses which we have studied thus far are brief, and how closely they are linked with definite historical situations. These latter would be impressed upon the mind of an eye-witness both by their inherent character and by the words to which they gave rise. All this has its bearing upon a theory of an origin of the gospel. In the first scene the Jews ask a question which "at this period of the ministry was inevitable" and which was expressed in language "exactly representing the real difficulties and hesitation felt" by them. The question is the outcome of the confusion of opinion resulting from miracles and teaching on one side and the non-fulfillment of their Messianic hope on the other.

SUB-DIVISION A—(22-30).

XII. Analysis of Address—(25-30).

Theme: THE WITNESS TO HIS MESSIAHSHIP.

I. He has given it to them more than once, 25 *a*.
They will not accept it, 25 *b*.

II. His works done in the name of the Father were part of it, 25 *c*.
They would not accept this witness, 26 *a*.

Reason: Because they were not His sheep, 25 *b*.

His sheep

(*a*) Hear His voice
(*b*) Are known by Him } (27).
(*c*) Follow Him

(*d*) Receive eternal life
(*e*) Shall never perish } (28).
(*f*) Are absolutely safe

(Proofs of verses 29, 30.)

XIII. Suggestions and questions for Study. 1. Name the seasons in Palestine and describe winter. (See B. D., Palestine, Vol. III, pp. 643, 644; Stewart, the Land of Israel, Chap. II.) 2. Give at least six of the Messianic claims Jesus had hitherto made before these Pharisees. 3. What does Jesus really mean by the reason He assigns in verse 26? 4. Is "eternal life" in John primarily a quantitative or qualitative term? (Gather instances by use of concordance and draw out an answer.) 6. Paraphrase verses 28-30 so as to bring out the truth given here in figurative form. 7. Is the doctrine of "final perseverance" taught in 27, 28? (See the careful note in Westcott in loco.) 8. Does the context justify an interpretation of verse 30 in a metaphorical sense *i. e.*, oneness of substance? 9. Is a Messianic claim such as Jesus made virtually a claim to Deity?

SUB-DIVISION B—(34-38).

XIV. Analysis of Address—(34-38).

Theme: THE JUSTIFICATION OF HIS CLAIM TO SONSHIP.

I. From the very wording of their own law, 34-36; (an áfortiori argument).

II. From the works which He had done, 37, 38.
(*a*) Had there been no works, no faith would be required, 37.
(*b*) Even with works, credence should be given to them, if (38 *a*) not to Him.
The purpose of this credence: "in order that," etc., 38 *b*.

XV. Suggestions and questions for Study. 1. To what is Jesus referring in verse 34, and give the exact force of "gods" here? 2. Write out in syllogistic form this argument. 3. Read Westcott's comment showing how this argument meets the charge of blasphemy founded upon the statement "I and the Father are one." 4. Does Jesus make here a direct appeal to His miracles? Can they justly be excluded from the appeal He makes to "works"? If they are to be included, what about the evidential value of the miracles? 5. If the Pharisees give credence to the works, what fundamental postulate of their theology are they brought to?

SUB-DIVISION C—(40-42).

This short section deserves critical attention for its evidence that an eye-witness is writing. Can we not discover in it these facts: (*a*) That the writer was originally a disciple of John the Baptist or that he had, at least, been with John? (*b*) That he knew the character of the Baptist's ministry? (*c*) That he carried in mind John's witness to Jesus?

XUI. Topic for Research. THE SON OF GOD: The origin of the phrase and its use by Jesus. Note—Verse 36 does not in the original read "the Son of God" but "a Son of God." This is, nevertheless, a good time to study the phrase. (See Stevens' Johannine Theology, Chapter V; Bruce's Kingdom of God, Chapter VII; Wendt's The Teaching of Jesus, Vol. II, pp. 122-137.)

Outline Studies in the Gospel of John,

BY

JAMES STEVENSON RIGGS, D. D.,

Professor of Biblical Criticism in Auburn Theological Seminary, Auburn, N. Y.

Prepared for the Rhode Island Committee of Pastors.

*Outline Study X.

CHAPTER XI.

THE RESURRECTION OF LAZARUS.

No chapter of the Fourth Gospel has been subjected to more criticism than this one regarding Lazarus. There are, therefore, two possible new points from which one may study it. One keeps in sight the theories made regarding its origin and character, and seeks to construct an apologetic for the whole story, the important considerations being the miracle and the literary structure. The other view-point keeps clearly in mind the central teaching of the chapter and works out from this to an understanding of the place, purpose, and significance of the event. The emphasis is not upon the miracle. This is always assumed in such statements as speak of it as "the climacteric miracle," and such emphasis requires an explanation of the omission of the story from the synoptics. The item of "four days" (v. 39) does not make this a greater miracle than the raising of the Widow's son at Nain. It is because of the teaching, not because of the wonderful character of the deed, that John gives us this account. The light of the whole scene but irradiates the declaration of Jesus, "I am the resurrection and the life." When John wrote he saw the significance of this claim as interpreted by the resurrection of Jesus Himself, and shall we not say by the theology of Paul. It is the climacteric "I am." The claim is superlatively Messianic. It contains within it the promise that life shall not only be called out of death, but triumphantly carried through it and beyond it to a deathless blessedness. In the hour when Jesus uttered these never-to-be-forgotten words He reached the height of His Messianic declarations. It is, therefore, from the view-point of this utterance that the chapter should be studied. If one wishes to work with the object of defence, it would be well to read first, Strauss, Renan, and Keim concerning the miracle, and Holtzmann and Wendt for the literary structure. The chapter contains a number of touches which reveal an eye-witness (see verses 3, 5, 6, 8, 16, 18, 20, 28, 31, 33, 36, 41, 44).

In regard to the whole presentation of Martha and Mary the words of Weiss (in Meyer) are worthy of note: "If these characters are altogether a fictitious creation we have a literary miracle of the second century." As in previous chapters, the development of faith and unbelief are both marked (45-53). We can with most convenience study the

---

*For Literature, etc., see Outlines I-III.

whole history by taking it according to its scenes and places, of which there are three,—one in the Peraea (1-16), another in Bethany (17-46), and the third in Jerusalem (47-53).

FIRST SCENE. In Peraea. Jesus, the Messenger from Bethany, and the Disciples. (1-16).

Before beginning with the text of this chapter it would be well to read Luke 11:1—17:10. After the Feast of Dedication Jesus "went away beyond Jordan," and all that we have of the Peraean ministry up to the time of the visit to Bethany is given us in the above Lucan section. Read also critically Luke 10:38-42. A good account of the Peraea will be found in Hastings' B. D. In this first scene four considerations interest us:

1. The three-fold issue of the sickness of Lazarus.
2. The singular delay of Jesus and its probable reason.
3. The misunderstanding and fear of the disciples.
4. The significant "day" and its demands.

I. **Suggestions and Questions for Study.** 1. Locate Bethany. 2. From all the notices given of her, estimate the character of Mary. 3. Make it clear that Mary of Bethany, Mary Magdalene, and the woman who annointed Jesus (Luke 7:37), are three distinct persons. Art has wrought much confusion concerning them. 4. How many annointings are recorded in the Gospels? 5. Does the message of verse 5 indicate frequent visits to this Bethany home? 6. Does the word of Jesus in verse 4 imply that He knew what He was to accomplish in Bethany? If so, how did He know it? 7. It is in this verse (4) that the difficulties of the chapter begin. Is the expression, "This sickness is not unto death" of double import, or is Weiss correct when he says that up to this time Jesus did not know whether He was to heal His sick friend or to raise him from the dead? 8. In the original the verb "loved" is placed in an emphatic position and through the connecting particle of verse 6 it is closely united with the statement "he remained," &c (6). Paraphrase this so as to bring out the full force. 9. Can you give any satisfactory conjecture as to why Jesus waited two days in the Peraea? Did not delay cause needless suffering? 10. To what event does verse 8 make allusion? 11. To what time does Jesus refer in the word "day" (9)? 12. If in this whole conviction regarding His safety Jesus is so sure, why had He left Judea before this? (See John 4:1). This question reflects upon your interpretation of the word "day." 13. Might it not have been possible that Jesus received another message prior to the statement of verse 11? 14. Does this chapter throw any light upon the fact that "sleeping" is really a euphemism for death? Can c. g. one be absolutely sure that the daughter of Jairus was really dead? (See Plummer: Internat. Crit. Com., in loco.) 15. Is it better to translate the last word of verse 12 "he will recover" or "he will be saved"? Why is the former better? 16. Show the logical relation of each clause in verse 15. 17. What, in general, was the character of Thomas? Make an inductive study from all the references to him in the gospels. 18. Can you give any instance from the life of Jesus when He created an opportunity for the display of power?

II. **Topic for Research.** The Burial Rites of the Jews. See Hastings' B. D., "Burial"; Tristram, Eastern Customs in Bible Lands, Chap. V; Stapfer's Palestine in the Time of Christ, pp. 165-171.

SECOND SCENE. At Bethany. Jesus, His friends, and the Jews. (17-46).

With the words "so when Jesus came" the scene is shifted and we find ourselves upon the pleasant hill-slope where Bethany stood amid olive trees and overlooking the deep valley which descends to the

Jordan. As preparatory to a study of the details of the story it would be well to get some idea of the Jewish belief in Christ's time regarding resurrection. (See for this, Charles: Eschatology, Hebrew, Jewish and Christian; Hastings' B. D., "Resurrection".) As central to the whole scene the teaching which Jesus gives merits just here a few words. Two relationships are included in the declaration "I am the resurrection and the lite ": (1) That of resurrection and life, which means I am the resurrection *because* I am the life ; *i. e.* resurrection is the result of life, its outcome ; its full expression. (2) That which is personal in the case of both resurrection and life, "*I am*" the resurrection. If you review Chapter V in the light of (1) you will see how these two realities are linked. You will see how easily in the conversation of this scene the expression "shall rise " is exchanged for "shall live." In view of these relations it were worth while to mark the points of difference between Christ's own resurrection and this of Lazarus. Lazarus did not bring "life and immortality to light "; Christ did. "The raising of Lazarus marks the highest point (not in the manifestation) but in the ministry of our Lord ; it is the climax in a history where all is miraculous—the Person, the Life, the Words, the Work. Here on the height the two ways finally meet and part, and from this high point we have the first clear outlook on the death and resurrection of Christ of which the raising of Lazarus was the typical prelude. From this height we have also an outlook upon the gathering of the church at his empty tomb where the precious words spoken at the grave of Lazarus received their full meaning till death shall be no more." Edersheim.

ÏÏÏ. Suggestions and Questions for Study. 1. Past what places of interest in Jewish history would Jesus go on His way from "beyond the Jordan " to Bethany? What was the general character of the way? 2. Does John refer to the same people as are spoken of in 10:33 when he speaks of the "Jews" in verse 19? 3. Why does Jesus tarry outside the village? 4. Estimate the character of Martha. 5. Does verse 21 contain a reproach? If not, what is its exact meaning? 6. Show how Jesus draws out the faith of Martha. 7. Is it likely that she understood what He said (25) ? 8. Do you think that Christ's redemptive work includes physical death? Answer this only after reflection and after carefully studying verse 26. Sanday calls our attention to the "readiness and unembarrassed vigor of Martha's answers, combined with a not very profound intelligence." In the light of this, read the confession of verse 27. It is an explicit, full recognition of Messiahship, such as was especially commended when uttered by Peter. Did Martha understand all she said? 8. The brief scene 33-44 is full of varied and intense emotion. Nearly every expression of it needs study. 9. We begin with "He groaned in the spirit." Study the uses of this verb in the N. T. (See Matt. 9 :30; Mark 1 :43; 14:5.) What was the reason for this deep feeling? 10. How do you make the tears of Jesus consistent with the clear knowledge that He would raise Lazarus. Is it possible that they were tears of sympathetic joy rather than grief? 11. The Greek N. T. uses two verbs for one English verb "to love." One denotes "love of the affections" illustrsted here in verse 36; the other is exemplified in Matt. 5 :44 and denotes "love of the will." 12. To what do the Jews refer in verse 37 ? 13. For a description of a Jewish tomb like this see Hastings' B. D., "Sepulchre." 14. It will be often found helpful to substitute for the word "glory " in the N. T. the word "manifestation." The word "glory " often leaves the thought too indefinite. Martha was to see here a manifestation of God. 15. Christ's prayer here takes the form of thanksgiving rather than petition. Why? 16. He implies, does He not, that He has asked? Is petition consistent with omniscience? 17. Just what was accomplished by giving thanks publicly? 18. Why the "loud voice" of verse 43? 19. What was the immediate effect of the miracle?

IU. Topic for Research. In what sense has Christ brought "life and immortality to light"? Other peoples before His time believed in life beyond death. What has He contributed to that belief?

THIRD SCENE. IN JERUSALEM. The Sanhedrin and Caiaphas.

This short section deserves study because of its fidelity to the historical situation in Jerusalem at the time when its scenes took place. The Pharisees were the guardians of the Messianic expectations. These expectations were largely the product of the sufferings and misfortunes of the Jews from the days of Antiochus Epiphanes. It was the duty of the Sanhedrin to see to it that no false prophet misled the people. In their eyes Jesus was doing just this. If He succeeded, the Sanhedrin would lose the very reason for its existence and nothing would prevent the Romans from having entire control. To men who thought thus, the conduct of Jesus, so utterly indifferent to political or national ideals was little less than high treason. His miracle-working only made Him the more dangerous. Such an act as the resurrection of Lazarus make their duty pressing. For nearly two years the Master had been watched. Reports of all His deeds and sayings had been carried to Jerusalem. The enthusiasm of the people had up to this crisis in Galilee, made these watch dogs of orthodoxy hesitate about action which might be too decided. That enthusiasm had turned after the feeding of the five thousand, but such miracles as this would quickly bring it back. "What are we doing"? is the self-reproachful question which reflects upon this whole situation.

U. Suggestions and Questions for Study. 1. To which party did the High Priests belong? 2. What was the general character of the priestly class in Christ's time? (See Schürer, Jewish People in the Time of Jesus Christ, Div. II, Vol. I, pp. 207-254; Stapfer, Palestine in the Time of Christ, 426-439.) 3. It is to be noted that what should have been proof of the righteousness of the claims of Jesus—(v. 11) "many signs"—becomes here the argument of blind fanaticism. 4. Show the possible inner historical connection of the condition and conclusions of verse 48. 5. Give some account of Caiaphas (see Hastings' B. D.). 6. The emphasis is upon that year. There is no historical inaccuracy here. It will repay the student to make himself acquainted with the history of the high priesthood among the Jews from the days of Jonathan Maccabeus. That history is one of the evidences of the nation's sufferings (see Schürer, Div. II, Vol. I, pp. 195-206). 7. Explain the policy of Caiaphas and show how it was virtually a prophecy. 8. The student of the Greek will note the preposition used in 50-52 and translated into English by "for"— "for the people." 9. The words of 52 are an extension of the principle set forth in 51. 10. Who are "the children of God" in verse 52? 11. The death sentence is the climax of all the espionage and plotting hitherto. 12. Jesus now carefully gets away from the neighborhood. How do you make this consistent with what He has said in 9, 10? 13. What deserts are found in Judea? 14. Where is Ephraim generally located? 15. It is of interest to know of the general preparations for the Passover (see Edersheim's The Temple and its Ministry, 184, 185). 16. Mark the situation depicted in 56, 57. Intense desire to see Jesus is mingled with fear owing to the determination of the authorities. This trying attitude is familiar enough to the student of the history of Judaism from 176 B. C. to A. D. 30. The Pharisees placed the people many times in just such perplexing positions. Indeed this whole Jerusalem picture amply justifies the words of Sanday: "It is rarely in ancient literature that we find a highly complicated situation so well understood and described."

UI. Topic for Research. What hints does the Gospel of John give us of a doctrine of Atonement? Compare also the First Epistle.

Outline Studies in the Gospel of John,

BY

JAMES STEVENSON RIGGS, D. D.,

Professor of Biblical Criticism in Auburn Theological Seminary, Auburn, N. Y.

Prepared for the Rhode Island Committee of Pastors.

* Outline Study XI.

CHAPTER XII.

The Threefold Relationship of Christ and a Review of Jewish Unbelief.

Between the events recorded at the end of chapter XI and the scene which opens chapter XII, a considerable time intervenes, the length of which cannot be accurately determined. Jesus was in the Perea, and we have the record of a small part of His teaching and healing (see Luke 17 : 11—19 : 28). The time had now come for His last journey to the capital. The "day," such as He had recently spoken of, was drawing to its evening, and He must accomplish what yet remained to be done before the cross should be set up. In this twelfth chapter we come to the end of the second great division of the Gospel. In events it is linked with the great solemn week which brought the end; in the feelings awakened it keeps in line with what goes before. It gives us the climax of the public ministry, and that climax shows us the same mistaken expectations, the same bitter antagonism, the same exceptional devotion. The light is brighter, the shadows deeper. In three striking pictures the author presents the relationships of Christ to the disciples, to the people, and to the outside world, and then follows a review of the antagonism which has now reached its climax in the sentence of the Sanhedrin against Jesus.

---

* For Literature, &c., see Outlines I-III.

The first part of the chapter contains a double picture of the position of Jesus in which He is presented as winning the affection and admiration of men at the very time that He is under the death-sentence of the Sanhedrin. Both pictures have over them the shadow of the hatred of the hierarchy; on both there is the expression of ardent homage. A moment's glance at the Synoptics will show that the chronological arrangement of events is not uppermost in the mind of the writer, for he has placed together scenes from the beginning and from the middle of Passion Week. It seems rather to be his purpose to show us the situation in Judea before we enter upon the events of the Passion. The resurrection of Lazarus was indeed critical in this situation. Because of it the " Jews " were now waiting their opportunity to arrest the Master while the people were being awakened to new enthusiasm. It was high time for the Sanhedrin to act if they did not wish to see the people carried away. Jesus henceforth walks and speaks openly. He knows how near the end is. Every scene is quick with tragic interest. There are all through the chapter the touches of an eye-witness, vivid and minute (see 2, 3, 8, 9, 18, 19, 22). The whole narrative falls naturally into four parts, and we shall take them in order.

PART I.—THE SUPPER IN BETHANY—(1-8).

The news of Christ's coming had undoubtedly gone before Him, so that when he arrived in Bethany preparations were on the way for a banquet in His honor. It is not without significance that Lazarus is especially mentioned. He is the constant reminder of that imperishable truth, "I am the resurrection and the life". The head of Jesus had at this time a price put upon it. Beside Him doomed to death sits the evidence of His power over death. Jerusalem in league against Him ; the very central fortress of evil vanquished. A feast over a resurrection at which there was to be an anointing for a burial. Such are some of the vivid contrasts that appear in that guest room in Bethany. The two significant moments of the evening were when Mary annointed the Lord, and when Judas spoke.

1. **Suggestions and Questions for Study.** 1. From what time are the "six days " usually reckoned ? (See Andrews', p. 344; also commentaries in loco.) Friday evening seems the best conclusion as to the time of the arrival. 2. Compare the account as given by the Synoptics, and note the particulars found in John which they do not give. 3. Discuss fully the description "ointment of Spikenard"; give the value of the ointments in dollars and cents. 4. In some recent literature the theory is advanced that Judas was ambitious rather than avaricious. How does verse 6 bear on this theory ? 5. The student of the Greek will note the imperfects in verse 6, and will also mark the two possible meanings of the verb translated "took away". 6. Do you think that Jesus knew what kind of a man he was taking when he chose Judas Iscariot to discipleship ? 7. Do you think that the

harsh judgment of verse 6 is made in the full light of all that was *afterward* revealed of the character of Judas, or was it an estimate of the disciples during their association with him? 8. Is there any reason whatever for the identification of this annointing by Mary with that given in Luke 7 : 36-50 ? Prove your answer. 9. The student of the original should critically examine the translation of verse 7. Strong external evidence is apparently in contradiction with internal evidence for the reading here. (See Dod's Ex. Greek Test. in loco.) 10. Why does the Lord make so much of this simple act of Mary? Do you think that Mary really had the intention here ascribed to her? Another has said: " Her quick sympathy with her Lord made her sensitive to the reality of that shadow of death and disaster that had settled down on His spirit and made a chill in the sunshine of His heart. So she went and prepared for that dark day a fragrant tribute of affection ". Is this interpretation justifiable?

II. **Topic for Research.** The character and aim of Judas. It greatly enhances the interest of this study to start with the supposition that Jesus knew him only in a general way and favorably when He selected him. Mark as far as possible the development of the man, estimating his motive from the scattered statements made regarding him.

PART II.—THE TRIUMPHAL ENTRY—(9-19).

Keim tells us that "in the face of the irritability of His opponents, in the face of the powerful means at their disposal for crushing Him with the speed of wind and the force of storm, there remained to Him but one chance, but one dreadful weapon—reckless publicity, the conquest of the partially prepared nation by means, not of force, but of idea, by the bold and complete unfurling of the clearly and loudly and—to the popular mind—eloquently speaking banner of that Messiahship, the secret of which He had so long hidden within Himself and of which He had held possession with growing certainty of victory notwithstanding all He had suffered. He staked His life upon the venture ". There is not an iota of evidence in any of the evangelists that Christ ever changed His idea of Messiahship. If Keim has said all that can be said of the Triumphal Entry, it was a poor, foolish, short-sighted venture. The crowd which shouted that day the equivalent for the modern "God save the King" was ready within four days to cry "Crucify Him ". The glory of the Bethany miracle filled the eyes of the multitude. The narrative keeps that in the foreground. Jesus for a brief time allows the people, while under the spell of that miracle, to proclaim His Messiahship, but their minds were upon other issues than His—He knew that. He was playing no bold game. He was acting consistently His part—choosing to ride to the city with no stately pomp nor worldly display. This is the same Messiah whom John has been presenting to us in one chapter after another. The scene is true to the spirit of all the gospels. Its symbols of peace and its signs of dominion had no quarrel to make with either Jew or Roman, except as righteousness and truth were withstood by evil or falsehood. John wishes us to see this as the disciples saw it when, after the ascension, they looked back upon the strange procession, interpreting it by words from the prophecy of Zechariah.

III. Suggestions and Questions for Study. 1. Compare critically the four accounts of this event and note what is peculiar to each. 2. What gave rise to the Triumphal Entry? (See Weiss, Life of Christ, Vol. III, p. 227.) 3. Do you think it was expected by Jesus Himself? Read carefully the accounts in the Synoptics before answering. 4. Do you look upon the procuring of the colt as a miraculous incident, or would you agree with Weiss that it is explained by the supposable fact that Jesus and His disciples were well known to the owner of the animal. 5. What was the real purpose of this formal entry? 6. Keep in mind the fact that it is John's gospel which tells us how this triumphal procession came to be. 7. Some interesting questions arise regarding the word of prophecy in v. 15: (*a*) What was the original application of the words? (*b*) Matthew says that the securing of the colt was " in order that " the word of the prophet might be fulfilled. Do you think that Jesus sent for the colt with His eye fixed upon this prophecy? The student of Greek will find it worth his while to study critically the " in order that it might be fulfilled," so often used to introduce O. T. prophecy. Any such study should be prefaced by a careful grammatical study of the Greek particle, translated " in order that ". (See Winer, Buttman, Blass, N. T. Grammars.) 8. As showing the Johannine presentation of this event note that the lamentation given by Luke is omitted, as also the request of the Pharisees. On the other hand, note how John's narrative accounts for the multitude that went *before* Jesus and the crowd that followed *after* in that jubilant procession. 9. What was the effect of the whole scene upon the Pharisees? 10. Bethphage has not yet certainly been indentified. The old road from Bethany to Jerusalem lay higher up on the Mount of Olives than the modern highway.

IV. Topic for Research. The extent to which Jesus intentionally fulfilled prophecy. This can be worked out in connection with a critical consideration of the question suggested in question 7, above.

PART III.—THE REQUEST OF THE GREEKS.

The selective character of John's narrative is here emphasized by the presence of this one event out of the many which occured between the Triumphal Entry and the Supper. The fact that it is the only recorded event from three busy days of teaching and working compels attention. It must have something significant about it. It was the kind of event that needed the full light of Christ's finished work and the spread of Christianity to give it full interpretation. As it stands in the Gospel, it requires considerable reading between the lines. In all likelihood its place in the order of events is correctly given in the Synoptics as, on the other hand, the correct position is given by John to the Supper at Bethany. As throwing light upon the request of the Greek ones, should bear in mind the cleansing of the Temple with its attendant teaching, "My house shall be called a house of prayer for all nations"; the intense, constant interest of the people; the impatient, malignant watchfulness of the authorities and the desire, according to tradition, that Jesus should leave the ungrateful Jews to take up his residence in some foreign land, where he might expect honorable welcome. The desire to see Jesus may have had a sort of "Come over to Macedonia" message behind it. Be that as it may, it gives the Master opportunity to set forth the way by which His going out to the world was to be accomplished. His words have over them the sharply-defined shadow of the cross. They give the vital necessity in order that a Messiah to the Jews shall be a spiritual Messiah to them and the world. They state what must be in order that a Hebrew Temple may become a universal sanctuary. Herein is their significance for the Fourth Gospel. The whole chapter brings out by its chosen pictures both the spiritual nature of the real Messiah and the "promise and potency" of the cross. Perhaps Pauline teaching gave imperishable importance to this third scene, in which the Greeks figure. Jesus makes three short addresses, which are of thematic character, showing that we have only an outline of what he said.

A. FIRST ADDRESS—(24-26).

Theme:—The Secret of Life's Glorification.

I. In Nature—dissolution, 24.
    (*a*) Processes. (1) Falling into the ground.
                     (2) Actual decomposition.
    (*b*) Result. Bearing much fruit.

II. In Personal Experience—hating one's life, 25. Note: Here the terms are equivalent to the conditions of nature.
    (*a*) Loving one's life—abiding alone.
    (*b*) Hating one's life—the outreach of the seed.
    Result. One keeps himself for "life eternal".

III. In Christian service—following Him, 26.
    Results: (*a*) "Where I am there also my servant shall be."
           (*b*) Him the Father will honor.

Upon this follows the incident of the voice from heaven, the perplexity regarding it and Jesus' word giving the reason for it. Then comes the second short address.

B. SECOND ADDRESS—(31, 32).

Theme:—The Significance of the Passion.

I. It is the judgment of the world, 31.
II. It is to bring about the "casting out" of the prince of the world, 31.

III. It will draw all men unto Him, 32.

These statements of Jesus suggest several perplexing questions to the bystanders. He does not answer their questions, but speaks upon their duty and privilege with respect to Him.

C. THIRD ADDRESS—(35, 36).

Theme :—The Duty in Reference to the Light.

I. To walk in it, 35,
    since (*a*) It is to be with them but a little while, 35.
          (*b*) Otherwise darkness may overtake them.
          (*c*) One walking in darkness knows not whither he is going.

II. To believe in it.
    Purpose. That they may become sons of light, 36.

U. Suggestions and Questions for Study. 1. These were Greeks, not Greek-speaking Jews, who came to Christ. How do they come to be present as worshippers at Jerusalem? 2. Distinguish between "proselytes of the gate" and "proselytes of righteousness". (See Hastings' B. D., "proselytes".) 3. Can you suggest any reasons why they went to Philip? Was Galilee in close relation with Greek-speaking peoples and Greek culture? (See Geo. Adam Smith's Hist. Geog. of Palestine, chapter XXVIII.) 4. Interpret fully the meaning of "see" in verse 21. 5. Give as full an account as you can of Andrew. 6. Show the relation of the answer of Jesus to the desire of the Greeks. 7. Just what do you mean by "glorified" in verse 23? 8. Does verse 24 imply by its figure vicarious sacrificial death? 9. What is the relation of the physical death of Christ to the spiritual blessing of others? In other words, how is the analogy of the seed to be understood in the spiritual realm? 10. Is it well, as you turn to the interpretation of verse 25, to remember that "self-culture and self-enjoyment were the master words with the Greek—the chief good of human life, the supreme aim, the ruling bent of the whole Grecian world". 11. No word in Scripture needs more careful exposition than the verb "hate." Does it express an attitude of the will or of the affections? 12. It will repay the student of the Greek to study carefully the word here translated "life". Is "eternal" qualitative or quantitative in force? 13. Note that through verse 26 "me" is emphatic. 14. Interpret the spatial relations in this verse, "follow", "be with", by spiritual equivalents. 15. Verses 27, 28 should be studied in parallelism with the Gethsemane experience (Matt. 26: 36-46; Mark 14: 32-42; Luke 22: 39-46). It is an anticipation of that scene and, as Godet says, shows us "just the reverse of that impassive Jesus attributed by criticism to St. John". Every clause of this brief section deserves critical attention. 16. The word for "tremble" is the same used in 14: 1. It points to a disturbance which takes hold of the very center of one's being. You will not feel the difficulty of the words which follow in verse 27 until you have read carefully the discussions of Godet and Reynolds. They differ in their interpretation of the interrelation of clauses. No interpretation should miss the intense humanness of this prayer. 17. In the matter of the voice from heaven, you must choose between the interpretation of Weiss, who eliminates the supernatural (see his Life of Christ, volume III, p. 248), and that which finds an experience similar to that recorded in Acts 9 :47 ; 22 :9. The narrative certainly gives the impression of a supernatural occurrence. 18. Verses 31, 32 suggest several significant questions: (*a*) Show how Christ's death was "the judgment of the world ". (*b*) Is " Prince of this world " a figurative expression or does it refer to a real definite personality? How is he to be cast out? (*c*) Is the meaning of "lifted up" exhausted by the crucifixion? (*d*) Does the "all men" of verse 32 mean universal salvation? If you think it does not, why not? 19. Note the importance all through this section of the death of Christ. Does it seem to you unlikely that Paul had emphasized for John the significance of this scene and the teaching accompanying it?

UI. Topic for Research. The date of Christ's death. It is well known that this date is in apparent contradiction to that suggested by the Synoptics, and has been used as an argument against John's Gospel. It is, therefore, of importance. See Aldrich's " The Day of Our Savior's Crucifixion " (a book worthy of careful consideration); Wendt's "The Gospel According to John ", p. 12 ; Introduction to commentaries of Godet and Reynolds ; Robinson's Harmony, notes to part VIII ; Wieseler's Synopsis of the Four Gospels, pp. 324-376.

PART IV.—A BRIEF REVIEW BY THE EVANGELIST—(37-50).

This section of chapter XII is instructive in two ways. It sets before us the causes of the unbelief which has all along been one of the main subjects of interest in the Gospel, and it shows us how the evangelist gathers together some of the main teachings of the gospel and puts them into the form of an address. Here is an instance where clearly Jesus did *not* deliver the address introduced by the words, " But Jesus cried out and said " (44). Verse 36 says that Jesus had "concealed himself". There is no indication of either occasion or locality for the words spoken. The student will note in them also a general character ; themes that have been before us in earlier chapters reappear. Too much should not be concluded from all this. The words are not fictions of the evangelist, though their arrangement is. Jesus at one time or another has said them. They are here introduced in this concrete way with strict truthfulness as to their source. The purpose in grouping them is to bring out clearly the responsibility of the Jews for the unbelief which is spoken of in the first section, 37-43. It is a clear instance where *subjectivity* appears in the use and arrangement of truths spoken on different occasions, but made serviceable by arrangement for a specific purpose of the evangelist. The passage falls naturally into two divisions, 37-43 giving us the cause of Jewish unbelief, 44-50 the responsibility for this unbelief and its seriousness.

UII. Suggestions and Questions for Study. 1. We meet in this section statements of real difficulty. Professor Toy, in his " Quotations in the N. T.", presents carefully the relation of the passage in Isaiah to the actual situation before the evangelist (see this, p. 88). 2. The commentaries say that we should not weaken the force of " in order that " in verse 38. Do you think the unbelief was in order to fulfil a prophecy? 3. In verses 39, 40 there is a setting forth of the relation of human inability and divine activity which requires careful thought. It is certain that God does not directly blind men's eyes nor harden their hearts. It is just as certain that He maintains the inviolable action of moral as well as physical laws. Man is free to use these laws to a good or bad end. We suggest an explanation along these lines. 4. Your understanding of verses 39 and 40 will be best shown by trying to make a paraphrase. How does the conduct outlined in 42 comport with the requirement found in Matt. 16:24? 5. The Jews believed, of course, in God. Note how, in verses 44, 45, Jesus makes God the ultimate in all matters of faith and spiritual insight. These statements give in summary what is taught in 6:38; 7:17, 18; 8:28; 10:38. For verse 46 see 3:19; 8:12. 6. As Jesus Himself in His character, conduct, aims reveals God, so what He has to say reveals God's mind. "I have not spoken", he says in verse 49, "from my own initiative"; God is the real author of all that I have said (49). The seriousness of the unbelief of the Jews was, therefore, in their inability, springing from moral perversity, to either *see* or *hear* the very God whom they, above all others, professed to worship. We would suggest that the student read just here the cogent words of Godet in his commentary on John, volume III, pp. 92, 93. 7. Conclude your study of the chapter by writing out all the Messianic claims to be found in it.

Outline Studies in the Gospel of John,

BY

JAMES STEVENSON RIGGS, D. D.,

Professor of Biblical Criticism in Auburn Theological Seminary, Auburn, N. Y.

Prepared for the Rhode Island Committee of Pastors.

Outline Study XII.

CHAPTER XIII.

Scenes Connected with the Last Supper.

With the beginning of this chapter we enter the third division of the Gospel. It is concerned almost entirely with the disciples. The passion of the antagonism which, in the chapters we have just finished is constantly evident, passes now, for a season, out of sight. The disappearance of Judas is, indeed, suggestive of its ceaseless activity, but in that upper room where they sat down to "supper," and where Jesus spoke, our interest is fixed and fascinated by revelations which present to faith a Messiah worthy of its fullest exercise. One critical question should have careful study before taking up the contents of the chapter, and that is the one suggested by the last topic for research in Outline XI—the date of Christ's death. Several questions are bound up with this, as *e. g.* the following: —Is this supper of chapter XIII the Paschal Supper, or is it entirely distinct, preceding the actual Passover meal by one day, and having another purpose in view? In addition to the references given in Outline XI, section VI, see Ellicott's Lectures on the Life of Christ, pp. 292, 293; see also the Cambridge Bible for Schools, John, Appendix A, p. 379. The chapter naturally divides itself into four parts: (1) A general introduction; (2) the scene of the washing of the disciples' feet (2-20); (3) the exposure and departure of Judas; (4) the word of Jesus after the Betrayer's withdrawal.

PART I. INTRODUCTION.

This is an introduction not simply to the scene which immediately follows, but to this whole division of the Gospel. As has been well said, "instead of being occupied with himself at this critical hour, when a terrible death was close upon Him, and instead of seeking help and comfort from those who were His disciples, He thinks continually only of the way by which He may serve and help them."

I.—**Questions and Suggestions for Study.** 1. For instances of like introductions in the Gospel see 2:23-25; 3:22-24; 4:1, 43-45. Godet's word is worth noting. This short introduction "is composed after exactly the same fashion as the chief prologue, its matter being entirely borrowed from the sayings of Jesus contained in the narrative which follows ". 2. What time is marked by the proposition "before" (1)? 3. What is the adverbial relation of the participle "knowing", *i. e.*, does it denote "though", or "because", or "when"? 4. Note how the significance of "the hour" is here defined. 5. What is the principal thought of this introduction? 6. Paraphrase the last clause of v. 1 so as to bring out the force of "having loved" and "loved". 7. Does "unto the end" denote time or intensity? (If possible, study the original.)

PART II. THE WASHING OF THE DISCIPLES' FEET. (2-20.)

If we combine the Synoptics and John, this scene may be given a two-fold introduction. One is found in Luke 22 : 24-30 ; the other in John 13 : 2, 3. Both serve to make clear the purpose and spirit of the act of Jesus. It is only as we keep close to the mental development and historical situation of the disciples that we can understand the unseemly contention which arose as they were going to the table. Edersheim's suggestion is worthy of consideration, that Judas started this strife. Some of the other disciples, however, were capable of it (see Matt. 20 : 20-28), but the favor of a seat of honor may have been part of the unblushing hypocrisy of Judas. It is no sufficient argument against this sad picture of selfish ambition as introductory to the washing of the disciples' feet, that John does not mention it. His words, as often, but deepen the motive of the Master. Luke tells us why, at this juncture, He stooped in humiliation to do this deed ;   n shows us the reach of His condescension. He who came from God, and who was about to go to God, performed this menial service. It is one of the evidences of the prefatory statement that " He loved to the end ".

II.—Questions and Suggestions for Study. 1. What do you understand by "the devil having already put it into the heart", &c. ? 2. Give the steps, as far as we know them, in the treachery of Judas. 3. What is the meaning of Iscariot? 4. To what does "all things " refer in v. 3 ? Do not give too broad an interpretation. 5. To what verb does the participle "knowing " of v. 3 belong? 6. V. 3 deserves careful study; it predicates an exalted consciousness in Jesus. 7. It would be well to keep before you in the study of the whole scene the aim to note all the touches which show an eye-witness. 8. What traits of Peter's character come out in this narrative? 9. In v. 7 Jesus promises Peter he shall know what He intends by this strange act. When does He tell him? 10. Interpret "unless I wash thee, thou hast no part with Me " (8). 11. Give first the literal meaning of the words in v. 10 ; then their spiritual significance. 12. It would make an interesting study to get at the meaning of the word "clean " as Jesus used it to the disciples in different places. It is well here to mark carefully the force of it. These wrangling, dull-witted disciples are now "clean ". 13. If you are a student of the Greek, mark the perfect tense in this whole section. 14. Do you see any reference whatever to baptism in all that we have gone over ? 15. Jesus now, in His interpretation, strikes at all hierarchical pretensions. 16. V. 15, in view of historical imitations of this very act, needs careful attention. Jesus does not say, " Do *what* I have done ", but " *as* I have done ". The words of Weiss are in point : " The example is not to be followed so much in its form as in its ethical substance and import ". It is well to note that when we seek to imitate the act of another we must consider two things : the act itself (including, of course, the spirit), and the environment of the act. Jesus would not make wine at a wedding feast in America. The pope does not really imitate Jesus by washing the feet of beggars in Rome. " Self-abasement to serve, and service to save ", are the spiritual realities here. 17. Note the value of experience as given in v. 17. 18. All through this section recurs the sad exception which Jesus is compelled to make. 19. Does " I have chosen " in v. 18 refer to "election to salvation " or has it a mere historical reference (see John 17 : 12) ? 20. V. 20 is to be connected with 16, 17, and shows another side of the relationship of the disciple and Master.

III. Topic for Research. Give the Ritual of the Passover Feast in Christ's time, and show its relation to the events of the Gospels. (See Edersheim, Life and Times of Jesus, Vol. II, pp. 490-512 ; Hastings' Bible Dictionary, Article " Passover " ; Stapfer, Palestine in the Time of Christ, pp. 440-446.

PART III. THE EXPOSURE AND DEPARTURE OF JUDAS. (21-30.)

Jesus had already given the false disciple hints of His understanding of the purpose that was to have such fatal issue. They were undoubtedly in order to invite Judas to depart. He did not take them, however, and now the Master proceeds to direct exposure. The account in the Fourth Gospel comes now into parallelism with Matt. 26 : 21-26 ; Mark 14 : 1, 18-21 ; Luke 22 : 21-23. The anxious question of the disciples shows how little the disciples really understood Judas. They certainly did not turn at once to him as the only man capable of such a dark deed. Judas had acted his part well. The account in Matt. 26 : 21-26 presents some difficulty when compared with John. If Jesus spoke so openly and decidedly as Matthew reports, then the disciples could not be at a loss as to why Judas departed. It is, perhaps, best to look upon the account of the Synoptics as condensed, presenting in a few sentences what is given in John in its true historic unfolding. Sanday's words are worth noting, for he says truly that in this episode of the discovery and exit of the traitor: "The Fourth Gospel is the fullest, the most minute, the most life-like, and the most intelligible ". It is simply impossible that any one but an eye-witness should have given in this way the varying situations of that critical hour when Jesus determined to banish from the upper room the one spirit which was not in harmony with its spirit and aims. As Godet remarks, John's account is "luminous, particular and exact ".

IV. Suggestions and Questions for Study. 1. Note the recurrence of the emotion which we first met in 11 : 33. It was a deep, soul-shaking horror which confronted Him as He looked through and beyond this betrayal, to all that it involved and signified. 2. Edersheim in his Life of Christ explains the seating at the table (see Vol. II, p. 494). The well-known picture of Da Vinci is entirely misleading. 3. Regarding the account which begins with v. 23, Sanday says : " This passage has a precision which is imperfectly preserved in the English version, e. g., the change of posture is emphasized and illustrated in the original by a change in each of the words, verb, preposition and noun. The exactness of this is wonderful". Attention is called to this, since a study of such details helps one to feel ultimately the "atmosphere" of this Gospel. 4. Just what do you understand by the expression, "Then Satan entered into him"? Does it indicate a different situation from that given in the words, "One of you is a devil" (John 6:70)?. It is, perhaps, a vivid way of describing a malignant disposition, or, in the former description, a resolution to commit murder? 5. Altogether the better order of events is that which places the departure of Judas before that part of the supper which we call the Lord's Supper. That was no place for traitors. 6. Show how the words regarding the disciples in v. 29 make a difficulty as to the time of this event. 7. Note the graphic touch, "and it was night".

U. Topic for Research. Is there a distinction in the New Testament between Demon-possession and Satan-possession? If so, what is it? Two different terms are used in the Greek, where one, "devil", is used in English. See on this whole subject, a recent valuable book by Wm. Menzies Alexander, M. D., B. D., entitled, "Demoniac Possession in the New Testament."

PART IV. THE WORDS OF JESUS AFTER THE BETRAYER'S WITHDRAWAL.

These verses are really introductory to the words which follow in chapters 14-16, and we shall so refer to them again. As the discourses themselves will fully occupy us in the next Outline, we give the study of these words here. It will be noted that vs. 34, 35 appear as a parenthesis in thought.

UI. Suggestions and Questions for Study. 1. Note carefully the tenses of the verbs in 31. One refers to the life of Jesus up to this moment; the other points forward to the events yet to be. Keep also clearly the distinction between the Son of Man and God. In what special sense has each been glorified? 2. Jesus had told the Jews (7:34; 8:21) of their inability to follow Him. Is the inability of the disciples founded upon the same reasons? 3. In what sense is the commandment to love one another new? Study carefully the context, and show how the command is to a richer, larger out-reach than is indicated in Lev. 19:18. 4. Do you think that Peter still thought of some form of material Messianic power and glory? 5. Note how his own confident assertion is met. Peter was prepared neither for the Messianic glory to which Jesus was going, nor for the martyrdom which finally would usher him into it.

UII. Topic for Research. Can you give any good reason why John omits the account of the supper? Can you find a suitable place for inserting it in this chapter? In general, discuss the question of the institution of the supper. What is the nature of the evidence which we have for its institution? Is the first account of the institution of it found in Paul? What is the relation of Paul's account to Luke's. Do Matthew and Mark in their accounts make it an institution? (See Harper's edition of Westcott and Hort's Greek Testament, Vol. II, p. 63; article in Expositor, 1899, Vol. I, p. 241, The Lord's Supper; St. Mark or St. Paul?; Hastings' Bible Dictionary, article, The Lord's Supper; Percy Gardner, The Origin of the Lord's Supper. For anyone reading German, the literature can be multiplied. See literature at end of article in Hastings' Bible Dictionary.)

Outline Studies in the Gospel of John,

BY

JAMES STEVENSON RIGGS, D. D.,

Professor of Biblical Criticism in Auburn Theological Seminary, Auburn, N. Y.

Prepared for the Rhode Island Committee of Pastors.

Outline Study XIII.

The Words of Jesus as Recorded in Chapters XIV—XVII.

For the study of these priceless chapters, the very heart of the Gospel, yes, the Holy of Holies of the New Testament, two methods of procedure are open to us. We may take them just as they stand and seek the connection as it seems to have been suggested to the mind of the writer or we may gather all the materials under certain general heads and make thus an entirely different arrangement from that given in the Testament; *e. g.* under the subject "the Paraclete" might be placed 14: 16, 17, 26; 15: 26; 16: 7-15 with such subdivisions as "His origin and character" and "His mission." If all the materials of the chapters were so arranged they might be placed under six general divisions:—(I) XIV: 1-27 (omitting 16, 17, 26), the objects of whose words is the comforting of disciples perplexed and saddened by the thought of their Lord's departure; (II) XIV: 16, 17, 26; XV: 26; XVI: 7-15 having for its general subject "the Paraclete"; (III) XV: 1-25, 27; XVI: 1-6 which speaks of the relation of Christ's disciples to Him and of the world to them; (IV) XVI: 16-23 which tells them that their sorrow shall be turned to joy; (V) XVI: 24-33, an epilogue; and (VI) XVII: 1-26, Christ's prayer. This method has the advantage of bringing together all that is recorded upon any given subject, thus securing unity and compactness. It seems to us, however, to break in upon the character of these addresses and in some measure to obscure the very naturalness of the reminiscences as they now stand. For, first of all it must be remembered that we have here the report of conversations and short talks which occupied perhaps two or more hours. More than once, in all probability, Jesus or the disciples came back to the same subject. It would appear now in one connection, now in another. It is an unlikely conception of the ongoing of affairs on that memorable evening to suppose that Jesus delivered a long formal address having complete logical arrangement. It is this view which has discovered in our present order of chapters marked "displacements." As Spitta's is the most noticeable illustration of it we give it here that the student may see what is involved. His order is 15: 1—17; 15: 18—16: 4; 16: 5—15; 16: 16—33; 13: 31 b—14: 3; 14: 4—26; 14: 27—31. It would be well to place the sections in this order and thus test the value of Spitta's theory, but it should not be forgotten that the aim of these chapters is to give *reminiscences* which shall make clear the "glory" of Jesus. We are thus brought close to the critical question regarding these chapters. How far do they bear a

Johannine impress? Do they contain the ipsissima verba of the Master? In order to an intelligent answer of such vital questions as these, some considerations must be borne in mind. (1) The style of the four chapters is uniform with that of the remainder of the book. We have here no more variety in manner of address than in chapter I or V. In so far certainly a Johannine impress is evident. (2) Questions about ipsissima verba are more or less associated with some form of a mechanical theory of inspiration. If after fifty years the Holy Spirit gave the apostle a definite memory of the exact words of Jesus, then, of course, the questions given above are easily answered, except as we are at a loss to know why the Johannine style is assumed, for it is surely present. The fundamental question then, is—Does the Holy Spirit work after this fashion? Does He not rather work in accordance with psychological laws? Does He not use given temperaments, peculiar training and given circumstances in order to secure the expression of truth as He will have it? And is truth less truth because it thus comes through the processes of human thought? If so, might it not be just to conclude that the Holy Spirit is of little service in all human utterances? Among the many things said that night in the upper room some were impressed upon the mind of the meditative apostle. These chapters show that he did not recall a great variety of subjects; nor does he remember a great deal about each subject. In the fourteenth chapter nearly all that he does remember centres about the questions asked. It is not unlikely that more questions were asked and that a process of selection is here to be supposed. Soon after that sad night came the Resurrection and light fell upon *all* the words Jesus had spoken. Through meditation and experience the Holy Spirit led the apostle into the innermost meaning of the teaching of the Master. John is not a short-hand reporter, nor does the Spirit make him one; he is an interpreter. Does interpretation always require ipsissima verba? The historical character of the scene, events, questions and personages is clear enough. The whole frame work of the discourses is unquestionably true to fact and the words themselves are *true to truth*. Why should we seek to go further than this? It is a serious question whether an attempt to do so does not imperil the whole gospel. As was said at the beginning the solution of the Johannine problem lies not in a demonstration of the continuity of external evidence in favor of John, but in the right appreciation of the *subjectivity* of the gospel. If it can be shown that, while it has a special form and method it is at the same time historical and truthful, in the large sense of the word truth, then all things considered, the authorship by John makes less difficulties than any other supposition. One more consideration. The truth here given us roots itself, all of it, in the divine-human personality of Jesus. It is not the clothing of an idea; it is the interpretation of an unique, historical person. Without *Him* it were simply impossible. As has been said before in these papers such truth as is here given is beyond human invention. It requires Jesus, the Jesus of the synoptics and of the earlier scenes of this gospel, in order to its adequate explanation both as to origin and character. It is only in form and arrangement, not in substance, that we find evidences of Johannine impress. It is but fair to the student that he should be referred to literature which shall present to him both sides of the discussion of the nature of these discourses. For one side he cannot do better than follow Westcott carefully; for the other we must refer him to the 3rd Vol. of Weiss's Life of Christ, p. 305, and, if conversant with German, to the last edition of Weiss's commentary on John (in the Meyer series).

PART I. COMFORT FOR DISCIPLES PERPLEXED AND SADDENED

BY THE THOUGHT OF HIS DEPARTURE. (XIV: 1-31).

This portion of the words of Jesus is, for the most part, in the form of question and answer. The thought advances by way of a difficulty suggested by one or another of the disciples. The comfort which he seeks to give, in each case, lies in the promise which He makes or in the direct word which He gives. In XIII: 33 Jesus tells them that He has only a little while with them and that they can not follow Him "now." This brings Him to the first promise.

I. The Promise of Reunion. They must believe Him and out of their faith draw abiding comfort when He tells them—
>> (a) That in the Father's house are "many mansions," 2 ;
>> (b) That He is going to prepare a place for them, 2 ;
>> (c) That He will come and take them to Himself, 3 ;
>> (d) That they know the way, 4.

This last statement brings out a demurrer from Thomas, 5, to which Jesus makes reply by saying:
> (1) I am the way (to the Father);—
>> (a) By being the truth;
>> (b) " " " life, 6a.
> (2) I am the only way to the Father.
>> Hence (6b)
>> (a) Knowing Him is knowing the Father.
>> (b) From that time they knew and had seen the Father, 7.

The assertion just made (b) perplexes Philip, who doubtless is thinking of some vision such as came in the Old Testament theophanies, and he immediately asks to be shown the Father, 8. Jesus meets this by repeating his former statement and then He makes a distinct advance upon it in this way:
> He that hath seen Me hath seen the Father, 9 ; since the Father is in Him and He is in the Father, 10. The proof of this is in
>> (a) His words. }
>> (b) His works. } (10)

Upon the basis of this assertion Jesus makes appeal to faith in view of
>> (a) His union with the Father (evident in life and word), 11a.
>> (b) His works, 11b.

The thought of works leads on to the second great comforting promise.

II. The Promise of Power. Which power is to issue from faith and obedience.
>> (a) Greater works shall they do because of His departure, 12.
>> (b) Their prayers in His name shall be mighty, that the Father may be glorified, 13, 14.
>> (c) To them who obey His commandments another Advocate shall come, the Spirit of truth, 15, 16.
>>> (1) The world cannot receive this Advocate, 17a.
>>> (2) The disciples shall have Him with them and in them continually, 17b.

Once more Jesus returns to the thought of His departure, 18, and makes them a third promise.

III. The Promise of Personal Manifestation. NOTE.—This refers directly to His appearance to them after His Resurrection. The entire conception of a coming of Christ in spirit is Pauline, 18-25. In regard to this personal manifestation He says three things:
>> (1) He tells them the time of its realization—after a little while, 19a. His resurrection life guarantees their eternal life, 19b.
>> (2) He tells them that this personal manifestation will throw light upon the mystical union of Father, Son and disciples, 20.
>> (3) He tells them what is the condition on their part for the continuance of that intercourse begun at the ressurection, 21.

Judas, like Philip, has his mind fixed upon another form of manifestation. He is thinking of a Messiah who shall be visible to friends and enemies alike; hence his question: "What has happened that we and not the world are to see Thee (22)?" Jesus replies in substance: Love, shown in obedience, is the necessary condition of spiritual revelation. Where this love is, fellowship with the Divine reveals ever more clearly both the Father and the Son, 23, 24. All this shall be made clear by the Spirit, 25. The fourth moment of comfort given in this chapter is

IU. His Bequest of Peace.

      (a)   This peace is *His* peace, 27a.
      (b)   This peace is given not after the manner of the world's giving.

The thought is now brought back to the opening words of the chapter, 27c, and from another point of view reasons are given for these sentences of exhortation.

      (a)   The Father is greater.
      (b)   His words have prepared them for what is to come.
      (c)   That the world may know that He loves the Father.

T. Suggestions and Questions for Study. 1. The full force of the word "troubled" should be sought for. 2. Give the four ways of interpreting v. 1. (See Westcott in loco.) 3. What is the exact meaning of the word "mansions;" does this word give any clue to the character of the other world? 4. What is involved in the word "prepare" (2)? 5. Is the "coming again" to be referred to the great "second coming?" 6. Do you think that the disciples upon the basis of these words could look for the "second coming" in their time? Did they expect it in their time? Look carefully into the epistles before answering this question. 7. Do you see in the statement of Jesus "ye know the way," 4, a rebuke? It would be well to get together just here statements from the previous parts of the gospel which would give Jesus a right to say to the disciples "ye know." The dullness exhibited in this chapter has its bearing upon the possibility of the theory of a resurrection which is simply the result of a constructive imagination. Thomas gave the actual status of the disciples' minds. 8. Verse 6 is worthy of careful study. It does not contain three coördinate statements (see analysis above). This verse cannot be understood until spatial relations can be translated into spiritual equivalents. Could you tell another how "to come to the Father through the Son"? Could you intelligently explain what "coming to Jesus" means? 9. It is unfortunate that our English version translates two different verbs in v. 7 by the same English verb "to know." 10. Do you think that Jesus revealed the "omniscience" and "omnipotence" of God? If not, in what attributes are we clearly to find God by "coming to know" the Master? 11. Paraphrase v. 10. 12. Does "from myself" in v. 10 mean "on mine own initiative" or "by mine own power"? 13. Does Christ claim independent power in working miracles? 14. Does Jesus, in v. 11, make direct appeal to miracles as evidence of His Messiahship? If so, what about expurgating miracles from the gospels? 15. From the book of the Acts, cite several proofs of the fulfilment of the promise in v. 12? Can this promise be made universal, or has it application only to the disciples? 16. What bearing has the reason given upon the statement preceding it in v. 12. 17. Is v. 13 a *carte blanche* for prayer? Prove your answer. 18. Can v. 14 be cited as a justification for expecting anything from God if we ask for it "in His name"? This word of Jesus has been often misused. 19. Is the "coming" of v. 18 the same as that of v. 3? 20. Is "behold" used in two senses in v. 19? 21. Paraphrase the verse so as to bring out the connections. The meaning lies quite below the surface. 22. Look carefully at the expression "in that day" in v. 20. Does "day" here denote the time of a dispensation?

23. In what way do you interpret in your own experience the words in v. 21, "I will manifest myself to him"? 24. What is the abiding, changeless condition of spiritual insight and blessing (see 23)? 25. What do you consider to be evidence of the manifestation of the Son or of the abode within of the Father? 26. Show, if you can, what the peace of Jesus really is. If we are to have His peace, we should know what is signified in His life. 27. Just what does Jesus mean by saying that the disciples should rejoice in His going to the Father because the Father is *greater* than He? A good discussion of this word "greater" will be found in Reynolds' commentary on John in loco. 28. Mark v. 30 as a proof of Christ's sinlessness. 29. Bring out the meaning of v. 31 by paraphrase.

II. **Topics for Research.** 1. Christ's Doctrine of Prayer. This should be studied in the light of His example as well as from His teaching. The synoptics should, of course, be used. 2. Christ's Positive Teachings regarding the other Life. He did not say much but what he did say is pregnant with suggestion. For the first topic see Stevens' Johannine Theology, Chap. XII, and the literature there cited.

PART II. THE RELATION OF CHRIST'S DISCIPLES TO HIM AND

OF THE WORLD TO THEM.

(XV: 1-27; XVI: 1-6).

I. THE RELATION OF CHRIST'S DISCIPLES TO HIM.

A. Set forth, *in general*, under the metaphor of the vine. The teachings are (1-4)—
    (1) The oneness of Christ and His disciples—in me.
    (2) The expected issue of that oneness—fruit.
    (3) The secret of fruit-bearing—abiding in Him.
B. Made *specific* by direct word to the Disciples, giving (5-17)—
    (1) In full the issue of "abiding" or of being "taken away," 5, 6.
    (2) The interpretation of abiding, 7-10.
    (3) The blessings accompanying this abiding.
        1. Power in prayer, 7, 16b.
        2. His joy, 11.
        3. His friendship, 14, 15.
II. The Relation of the World to the Disciples—It hates them as it has hated Him, 18.
    (a) Reasons for this hatred.
        (1) The very opposition of nature, 19.
        (2) Ignorance of the Father, 21.
    (b) The inexcusableness of this hatred.
        (1) The word He had spoken left the world without excuse, 22.
        (2) The works He had done put them in the same position, 24.
        (3) They (*i. e.* the world) really hated without cause, 25.
        (4) The Holy Spirit and the Disciples shall bear witness to the fact that this hatred of the world is ever inexcusable, 26, 27.
    (c) The manifestation of this hatred—The disciples shall be put out of the synagogues and even killed (XVI: 2).
        (1) The motive behind all this, 2.
        (2) The real reason for their action, 3.
The consolation which with all this Jesus seeks to give His disciples appears constantly in the rich promises made to them and in the direct words of cheer such as are found in 15: 14-16; 16: 1, 4.

III. Suggestions and Questions for Study. 1. What is the exact meaning of "true" in v. 1? Is the figure of the vine used of Israel in the Old Testament? 2. What is the meaning of the expression "My Father is the husbandman." Is the whole relation of Christ and His disciples referable to the Father? 3. Note carefully the force of "in me." The whole figure suggests "vital union." How can one who has come into this "vital union" be taken away? The case of the disciples *and Judas* is here in joint. 4. The whole subject of the culture of the vine should be looked into. 5. In what sense were the disciples "clean"? How did the word make them clean? 6. The understanding of this whole section centres in a correct spiritual understanding of the word "abide." It should be carefully noted with all its modifying clauses. 7. Note changes which appear: "I abide in you," "my words abide in you;" and then, "abide in me," "abide in my love." There is here a continually closer definition of abiding. Follow it. 8. Note carefully again how the "ask whatsoever ye will" is tied up to the "if my words abide in you." The promises of Jesus regarding prayer must be understood in their context. 9. Note that in this section the strong word for love is used—a love which is an expression of will as well as of affection. "Obedience" and "abiding" become identical. 9. Note the expression "my joy." What evidence can you give that Jesus was a man of joy? 10. Do you see the connection between verses 11 and 12? 11. What is the signal difference between "friends" and "servants" as here given? 12. To what does Jesus refer in the words "all things that I heard from the Father," &c, 15? 13. Does v. 16 give us a statement of election to service? 14. Note again the connection of the statement regarding prayer in 16. 15. What does "of the world," 19, actually mean? 16. Give the exact force of "know" in v. 21. 17. Paraphrase v. 22 so as to bring out its full meaning. 18. Does "hate" all through this section refer simply to intense feeling? 19. Is the reference to works again a reference to miracles? 20. Why does Jesus say "they have seen and hated both me and my Father" rather than "have seen my works"? 21. Was expulsion from the synagogues a severe experience for a Jew? 22. Note the unsafety there may be in following an unenlightened conscience (2). 23. Note how often Jesus carries back the difficulty to an ignorance of the real nature of the Father? Do you think that theology yet needs a deeper knowledge of the Father? 24. Give the force of the reason found at the end of v. 4 in chapter 16. 25. Is the statement of v. 5, "no one of you asketh me whither goest thou," correct in view of what is given in 14; 5? Does this question argue for a displacement?

IV. Topic for Research. Is XV: 1-6 an Old Testament parable worked over into its present form by John himself? See Westcott on one side; also Godet; and Weiss (on John) on the other.

PART III. THE MISSION OF THE SPIRIT. (XVI: 7-15).

I. To the World.
    (a) To convict it of sin because it does not believe in Christ, 8.
    (b) To convict it of righteousness because Christ is gone to the Father, 10.
    (c) To convict it of judgment because the prince of this world is judged, 11.

II. To the Disciples.
    (a) To guide into all truth, 13,
        since (a) He shall not speak of Himself.
        (b) He shall speak only what He hears.

(b) To declare things that are to come.

(c) To glorify Christ by interpreting Him and His words to them.

U. Suggestions and Questions for Study. 1. What is the exact force of the word transliterated into English as "Paraclete?" Does it mean "comforter" or "advocate" or both? Note the bearing of the word "another" (wherever it occurs) upon the interpretation. 3. In 15:26 the Spirit is called "the Spirit of truth" (so 16:13). What does the phrase exactly mean? Paraphrase the expression so as to bring out its full force. See John 4:6 for its opposite. 4. In what sense was it true that if Jesus had not gone away the Spirit would not have come? Has not the Spirit always been in the world? 5. Vs. 9, 10 deserve careful study. The interrelation of the work of the Spirit and the reason assigned, in each case, should be carefully thought out. 6. Why is unbelief in reference to Jesus the crowning sin? 7. Is it the historical Jesus or the essential Christ that is here referred to or both? 8. What has "going to the Father" to do with a conviction of righteousness? 9. When in the life of Christ did the judgment of the prince of this world begin? Have we the Pauline sense of righteousness in v. 10? 10. In the Greek of v. 14 there is a perfect "is judged." Why? 11. Does the first part of v. 12 state a general principle of revelation in divine things? 12. How do you limit the expression "all truth" (13)? 13. Note in v. 13 that the same expression "from his own initiative" is used of the Spirit as has been used in reference to Jesus (5:19). There is a remarkable interrelation of Father, Son and Spirit, set forth in this gospel. 14. Godet sees in the last part of v. 13 the guarantee for the Apocalypse. 15. Can the church claim this promise for its own use today? If not, does the whole section belong to the disciples alone? In other words, have we no right to look for further light upon, say, the subject of Eschatology? 16. What is the inner relation between vs. 15 and 14? We suggest here reflection upon two statements of Weiss. (1) In this short section (5-15) is gathered together all that Jesus ever said about the sending of the Spirit and through the remembrance of what is given us in 5-7 the summary is made part of the farewell discourse. (2) The manner in which these promises of the Paraclete are given, offers us really the key to the whole treatment and reproduction of the discourses of Jesus in this gospel. Do you agree with these statements?

UI. Topic for Research. 1. The Personality of the Holy Spirit; also His office and work. An interesting phase of this study would be the comparison of John with Paul. See for the latter the four great epistles—Rom., I and II Cor., Gal. 2. Is Inspiration to be interpreted in a technical way and limited to the writers of the books of our Sacred Canon, or is the Spirit's influence yet active in inspiring men?

PART IV. THE JOY OF THE DISCIPLES ON THE RESURRECTION MORNING.

(16: 16-23).

    I. It shall come after a brief interval of deepest sorrow, 20.

        (a) Like a mother's joy over her new-born child, 21.

        (b) Because they shall see him again since He is going to the Father, 16, 22a.

    II. It shall be theirs forever, 22b.

    III. It shall be made complete since the Father would give them whatever they asked for their mission.

VII. Suggestions and Questions for Study. Commonly this section is supposed to refer to the parousia of Christ and the "seeing etc.," to spiritual vision. See if an adequate interpretation is not given by referring it to the Resurrection of Jesus? 1. Is not the Resurrection of Jesus the beginning of His "going to the Father"? 2. Mark again the slow perception of the disciples. It is a stubborn fact for all views of the resurrection which presuppose a psychological preparation for it on the part of these perplexed and saddened men. 3. The varied feelings set forth in v. 20 all had realization in those few days which compassed the Crucifixion and the Resurrection. 4. The clue to the interpretation of v. 23 is in the word *me*. It has an emphatic position and is in contrast with "the Father" below. 5. Note again the phrase "in my name" as essential to the interpretation of v. 23. 6. Why had they hitherto asked nothing in His name? 7. Have we here again an unlimited promise with reference to prayer?

PART V. AN EPILOGUE CONTAINING WORDS BOTH OF COMFORT AND WARNING.

(16 : 24-33).

I. As regards their future clear enlightenment regarding the Father, 25.

II. As regards their method of praying. It will be directly to the Father in His name, since the Father loves them
(*a*) because they have loved Him
and (*b*) because they have believed that He (Jesus) came forth from the Father.

To this last word is added the declaration of the character of His mission, 26, and the glad insight of the disciples regarding it, 29, 30.

III. As regards their panic-stricken desertion of Him, which shall leave Him alone and yet not alone since the Father is with Him, 32.

IV. As regards their peace in *Him* and tribulation *in* the world, 33a, b.

The address closes with an inspiring word—" Be of good cheer, I have overcome the world,"—33c.

VIII. Questions and Suggestions for Study. 1. What is the reference of "these things" in v. 25? Commentators differ about this. The end of the verse seems to refer specifically to things about the Father. With what do you connect the reference? 2. Did Jesus generally speak to the disciples "in parables" or "proverbs?" 3. Does the future enlightenment refer to the work of the Spirit? Can Jesus say "I" meaning thereby "I" through the Spirit? 4. Give the exact force of the last part of v. 26? Godet says that intersession on Christ's part is implied, if needed ; Weiss says that intercession is shut out altogether. Which is right? 5. For what does "for" in v. 27 give the ground or reason? 6. Give the different moments in the redemptive activity of Christ indicated in v. 28. 7. Do you clearly see how the disciples could say (29) " Now thou speakest plainly." If so, set it forth. 8. Does the "overcoming the world" refer to the death of Jesus (in which case, of course, He speaks proleptically), or does it sum up His whole triumph over sin in His earthly experience including death?

IX. Topic for Research. The mental attitude or situation of the Disciples just prior to the Crucifixion. We would suggest a careful review of the incidents succeeding the confession of Peter at Caesarea Philippi with the object of discovering whether or no the disciples so understood Jesus or so grasped the meaning of His Redemptive method, that they themselves could develop a resurrection doctrine, even though no actual resurrection took place. In other words get clearly before the mind the psychological development of the disciples during the last few months of Christ's ministry. The questions in these discourses will be of service thereto.

PART VI. THE PRAYER OF JESUS.

(17:1-26).

It was Luther's judgment that nowhere else in Scripture, nor indeed in the literature of any people, is there anything that can be compared with this prayer in simplicity, depth, grandeur and devoutness. The more fully we understand the life of Jesus and His Spirit, the more shall we comprehend the far-reaching petitions which He here offers. It seems well-nigh out of place to call attention to critical objections made against the transmission of the prayer to us by John—as e. g., the use of "Jesus Christ" in v. 3, the full doctrine of pre-existence (5, 22, 24). As an offset to such objections, we ask the student to consider carefully the words of Weiss: "Johannine phraseology and views are more deeply imprinted upon this prayer than upon any other passage. Notwithstanding this, however, we have here, too, such vivid reminiscences of what was spoken during that sacred hour, that only prejudice against the Fourth Gospel could suppose that this was a free composition by the evangelist." The prayer falls into three parts. We subjoin an analysis of these parts.

THE PRAYER OF JESUS. (XVII).

I.—For Himself—Glorify Me, I.

    (*a*) The grounds of the petition.
        (1) His hour had come, 1.
        (2) His work was finished, 4.
        (3) He had received power over all flesh to give eternal life, 2 ; definition of eternal life, 3.
    (*b*) The measure of the petition—with the glory which I had with Thee, 5.
    (*c*) The purpose of the petition—in order that the Son may glorify the Father, 1.

II.—For His Immediate Disciples—Keep them in Thy Name, II.

    (*a*) The grounds of this petition.
        (1) They know that all things which Thou hast given Me are from Thee, 7.
        (2) They have received the words I have given to them, 8.
        (3) They have believed that Thou has sent Me, 8.
    (*b*) The two-fold content of this petition.
        (*a*) Sanctify them by the truth, 17.
        (*b*) Keep them from the evil one, 15.

III. For Those Who Through the Disciples' Word Should Believe on Him.

    I.—That they may be one as we are, 21. The two-fold purpose of this.
        (*a*) That the world may believe that Thou hast sent Me, 23.
        (*b*) That the world may know that Thou hast loved them, 23.
    II.—That they may be with Me where I am, 24. The purpose of this: that they may behold My glory, 24.

Note.—The above analysis aims to bring out only the salient parts of the prayer. The interrelation of subordinate thoughts will receive attention in the suggestions and questions for study.

X. Questions and Suggestions for Study. 1. Weiss maintains against others that the first part of the prayer ends at v. 8 instead of v. 5 ; consider this. 2. The root meaning of the word "glorify" is "to make manifest." Using this meaning of the word, what manifestation is here asked for? 3. What is the relation in thought of v. 2 to v. 1? 4. Show why "glorification" was necessary to the exercise of His "authority over all flesh." 5. Do you find the doctrine of predestination in v. 2? 6. V. 3 is clearly an addition of the evangelist, and must be always kept in mind by one who objects to all statements of a Johannine impress upon this prayer. Surely Jesus did not stop in His praying to give a definition of eternal life. 7. In this definition occurs the verb "to know," which the student would do well to study in Cremer's Biblico-Theol. Lexicon. See also Thayer's Lexicon under this word, or Vincent's Word Studies (in loco). 8. In v. 4 it is better to take "having accomplished" as a participle defining the manner of "I have glorified." 9. Is Jesus speaking proleptically here or is He referring simply to all that activity which had occupied Him? 10. Do you think that Jesus had as clear a consciousness of His preexistence as is here indicated? If so, how did He come to it? Would you allow that Jesus learned this deepest secret of His being through the teaching of the Spirit? Much is involved in your answer. If you can read German, we would suggest a careful reading of Baldensperger's "Das Selbstbewusstsein Jesu" (it has recently appeared in a new addition). 11. Is v. 6 a part of the "I have accomplished the work, &c.", of v. 4, or does it mark a transition in thought to the prayer for the disciples? 12. What is understood under "Thy name" in v. 6? 13. Does v. 6 contain the doctrine of predestination? Attention is called to these statements, for they are used in Dogmatics as supports of this doctrine, and the question is whether exegetically they can be so used. 14. In v. 7 the Greek aorist can be translated "they have come to know." 15. What is the connection between vs. 8 and 7. 16. Note the emphatic position of "I" in v. 9. The "I" is the first reason for the hearing of His prayer. 17. "I pray not for the world" implies no casting off of the world, as has sometimes been said in the interest of Dogmatics. 18. Do you see the inner relation between 9 a, b, c? 19. Just what does "in Thy name" (11) mean? 20. If you are inclined to see predestination in this chapter, bear in mind that *one*, whom God had given Jesus, *was lost* (see v. 12). This is clear proof that Jesus, all through, has been speaking, not dogmatically but historically— a large difference for the understanding of these words about "giving," &c. 21. Again note that Jesus, though described as a "man of sorrows," was also a man of joy. It were interesting to study His life to find out its secrets of joy. Art has devoted itself almost exclusively to depicting Him as a "man of sorrows." 22. A noted preacher once said, "it is the nature of godliness to irritate ungodliness" (see 14). 23. What meaning can you give to "sanctify" which will make it apply both to the disciples and to Christ? also make clear how Jesus sanctified Himself. 24. What is the modus operandi of "sanctification by the truth"? 25. What kind of oneness is here spoken of (21)? 26. What was the "glory" which Jesus gave the disciples (22)? 27. Is the purpose expressed in 22 a mere repetition of that given in 21? 28. What is the force of the reason in the connection in which it stands for "Thou lovedst," &c? 29. Paraphase vs. 25, 26, so as to bring out their full force.

XI. Topics for Research. What is the eschatology of these four chapters? Can you frame their suggestions into a definite teaching.

Outline Studies in the Gospel of John,

BY

JAMES STEVENSON RIGGS, D. D.,

Professor of Biblical Criticism in Auburn Theological Seminary, Auburn, N. Y.

Prepared for the Rhode Island Committee of Pastors.

Outline Study XIV.

CHAPTERS XVIII, XIX.

Again, in Chapter XVIII, the writer comes back to narrative, and all those characteristics of his method of narration which we have heretofore noticed appear in his story. As introductory to our study, the following considerations deserve attention : (1) There is abundant evidence of an eye-witness (see vs. 1, 3, 6, 10, 11, 13, 15, the whole account of the denials of Peter, and v. 28). An eminent jurist has said of the transactions before Pilate that the writer of the Fourth Gospel has given us a remarkably faithful picture of its ongoing, *i. e.*, faithful in the clearness and naturalness of its changing situations. Chapters XVIII and XIX afford, therefore, an excellent field for the examination of the historicity of the writer. (2) There is evident, also, again, a selection of events. The general purpose of the Gospel, as we have already seen, is to exhibit the "glory" of Jesus, the Messiah. Here we are to see, as far as the arrest and trial are concerned, the complete voluntariness of the surrender of Jesus to His fate. Amid all the forces that combine to bring about His death, He stands Master, *i. e.*, He emphasizes the fact that He goes willingly along the dark way to which they have brought Him. Judas kisses Him, but He immediately offers Himself to the officers ; Pilate threatens, and is non-plussed before the dignified, unresisting sufferer. (3) When compared with the Synoptics, the account presents difficulties which may be compassed in two ways : one by that method of harmonization which is given in the harmony of Stevens and Burton ; the other, that exemplified by Weiss in his commentary on this Gospel. The former, *e. g.*, puts the order in this way : arrest, appearance before Annas, appearance before Caiaphas, during which occurred the denials of Peter, the assemblage of the Sanhedrin ; the latter : arrest, appearance before Annas, during which occurred the denial of Peter. John here really corrects the Synoptics, who knew nothing of a trial before Annas. It is always well to bear in mind that the Synoptics are not historians in one sense of the word ; nor is John, either. It is, therefore, possible for events to appear in just such varied relations. This question, therefore, may arise—which gives the more likely order ? Let the student examine both methods of meeting the difficulties and decide after carefully weighing the opinions on each side. It should be added that the facts by either method are brought to light ; only their interrelation is differently conceived. The narrative as given by the Synoptics should be kept in view.

THE ARREST. (XVIII : 1-11.)

1. **Suggestions and Questions for Study.** 1. Give the location of the Kidron and what is to be said of the site of the Gethsemane now shown to travelers (see Stewart, Land of Israel). 2. What are we to understand by "the band"? Why were soldiers taken along? 3. Just where in this narrative may we find place for the kiss of Judas? 4. Do you explain the "going backward and falling to the ground" as the result of some miraculous act? 5. Who are "they" in this connection? 6. Of course in the scenes about to be given, the deepening malevolence of unfaith is depicted. It would be well to mark it. 7. Note the description, "Jesus, the Nazarene," and its use in the first part

of the Acts. 8. Note carefully the points in which John's narrative differs from the Synoptics in the matter of Peter's rash use of the sword (10-11). 9. Note in v. 11 the fine self-surrender referred to in the introduction.

THE HEARING BEFORE ANNAS AND THE DENIAL OF PETER.
(XVIII : 12-27.)

II. **Suggestions and Questions for Study.** 1. Who was Annas, and what reason may be given for taking Jesus to him? 2. Give, in brief, a history of the high priesthood from the days of the Maccabees on (see Schürer, Jewish People in Time of Jesus Christ). 3. Can John be shown to be incorrect in his account of Annas or of this preliminary hearing before him? 4. Professor Sanday declares that " the interview in vs. 19-24 was held before Caiaphas " because of the use of the term " high priest " in 13 and 14. This compels him to read " had sent " instead of " sent." Weiss contends that the verb has its natural force and that the hearing was before Annas. Which is right? You will, of course, understand that according to the former interpretation the denials of Peter were while Jesus was before Annas; according to the latter, while Jesus was before Caiaphas. Renan says of the account in John of these denials that it exhibits a superiority to that of the Synoptics in that all is more circumstantial and better explained. It would be well, in view of such testimony as this, to compare carefully the two accounts and thus to get a clearer impression of the character of John's narrative as that of an eye-witness. 5. Just what is meant by " high priest of that year " in v. 13? 6. Have we any clue to the reason why the " other disciple " was known to the high priest? What explanations have been given? 7. Are we to see in the officers members of the Roman cohort, or had this been withdrawn? 8. Mark again the detail of an eye-witness in this scene—the porters, the several persons about the fire, the kinsman whose ear Peter cut off. 9. Note the general character of the questioning of Annas. He was feeling his way toward the grounds for an effective legal process, the supposition being that Jesus was the leader of some sort of secret society. 10. Weiss remarks with truth that the insult to Jesus (v. 22) would not be likely in a public sitting of the Sanhedrin. 11. Vs. 25-27 continue the account begun in v. 17. 12. Godet resolves the apparent contradictions of the Synoptics and John as to the place of the denials by supposing that Annas and Caiaphas inhabited the same sacerdotal palace. What do you think of this? 13. Note that John alone gives the occasion of the third denial. 14. What result came from the hearing before Annas? 15. Note that the time of the second cock crowing was about 3 o'clock in the morning, *i. e.*, at daybreak.

THE HEARING BEFORE PILATE. (XVIII:28—XIX:16.)

John simply alludes to the hearing before Caiaphas; he gives us no account of it. Nor is anything told us of the "assembly of the elders," referred to in Luke. We are taken immediately from the proceedings before Annas to the palace of Pilate. The conduct of Pilate affords a fine psychological study of the battle in a man's soul between conscience and the fear of public opinion, or, perhaps, selfishness as threatened by public opinion. Pilate is true to the picture which Josephus gives us of him. Indeed, without John's account, we should be at a loss to explain some of the situations given us in the Synoptics. As he gives the story, there are four distinct stages in it, marked off respectively by the verses 28-32, 33—XIX:6, 7-12a, 12b-16. Again, we shall find remarkable fidelity to the historical situation in Judea, as we know it from other sources. It will also be noted that it is in this Gospel alone that we have the record of the private examinations before Annas and Pilate. Westcott makes the likely supposition that John was present in each case. Some of the difficulties in these narratives call for especial research (see below).

III. **Questions and Suggestions for Study.** 1. Why did the Jews take Jesus to Pilate? 2. What was the business of a procurator in Judea? 3. How were Roman provinces in general governed?

(See Mommsen's Roman Provinces; also Schürer.) 4. Where was, probably, the location of the pretorium in Jerusalem? 5. Do you think that v. 28 means that the eating of the Passover lamb had not yet taken place? or do the words "eat the Passover" refer to the "chagigah" or peace-offering? 6. How had Pilate generally treated the Jews? (See Josephus—J. W. II, 9. 2-4; also Antiquities.) 7. Note the way by which the Jews at first avoid a specific charge. Why was this? 8. When did the Jews lose the right of putting a man to death? You will recall that Stephen was killed by them. 9. Were the Jews themselves intent upon crucifixion? You will note that John seeks wherever possible to show that the words of Jesus were fulfilled. With the refusal of Pilate to take up the case, the first stage of the examination comes to an end. Pilate now enters the Pretorium, taking Jesus with him. V. 33 in John presupposes Luke 23 : 2. "It is entirely after the manner of John to take for granted as understood that the only possible charge of any value before the governor would be high treason." 10. Just what is the intent of Jesus' question to Pilate (34)? Did it make any difference whether Pilate or the Jews used the word "King"? 11. Note that after what is said in v. 36, Jesus confessed to kingship. Could Pilate follow Him in His interpretation of His position? 12. What is the mood which asks "what is truth"? 13. Note that this conversation really gives the reason why Pilate was so anxious to free Jesus. The governor saw clearly that the Man before him had no political designs. Instead of following his own judgment, he turned to expedients. 14. Show that in the cry for Barabbas the Jews flatly contradicted themselves. 15. Is robber to be taken in the common English sense? 16. Do you think that there were two scourgings in the course of the sufferings of Jesus? It is well to remember that it was the preliminary to crucifixion, and John is strictly correct in his placing of this bit of suffering (see XIX : 1). Pilate evidently hoped that this severe measure would satisfy the people. It is to be noted that Pilate did not cause the mocking described in 2, 3. 17. Is this cry for crucifixion (19 : 6) the first that has been heard during these shameless proceedings? Look carefully at the Synoptics. Did the people have no part in it? 18. Could Pilate give to the Jews the right to crucify? If so, why did they not accept it? 19. Why did Pilate suddenly find himself again perplexed? A psychological experience here comes to light which is well worth examining (7, 8). 20. Note now that Jesus is silent. Why? 21. Who is the "he" of v. 11? This scene brings out again the voluntariness of Jesus, and 12a brings us to the close of the third stage in the story. In the last stage the priests push their last effective claim—their right to appeal to Cæsar. 22. Why did Pilate fear this? 23. Give in full a description of the mental dilemma of the governor and the way he resolved it. In other words, make a paraphase of 12-16 so as to bring out the mental processes of Pilate. 24. Which is right as to the specification of time—Mark (15 : 25) or John (19 : 14)? Can both be right? According to what method is time reckoned in John, the Roman or Jewish? 25. Why does John pass over the episode with Herod? 26. What facts in reference to Jesus appear in these trials?

IU. Topics for Research. 1. The Date of the Crucifixion of Jesus. This has been used as a fact arguing against the historicity of John. It demands, therefore, careful attention. We recommend the following method of study: get together all the data from the Synoptics and John bearing upon the matter. Understand distinctly just the point at issue and then seek a conclusion either through some method of harmonization or by deciding between the two presentations. Help will be found in all the introductions to the gospel. In addition to these see Wieseler, Synopsis of the Four Gospels; Robinson's Harmony; Aldrich, The Date and Day of Our Lord's Crucifixion; Hastings' Bible Dictionary. It would not be surprising if you should conclude that John is correct.

II.—The Illegalities in the trial of Jesus. There are repeated violations of Jewish law, and, of course, Pilate committed a gross violation of Roman law. (See Stalker's Trial and Death of Jesus ; Bible Dictionary and literature there cited.)

THE CRUCIFIXION AND DEATH. (XIX : 17-30.)

As introductory to this scene, two subjects are worthy of considerable attention. (1) The Roman method of crucifixion. No one can fully appreciate the horrors of this manner of putting men to death until he has acquainted himself with the brutality, torture and shame attending it. Fever, slow death and insanity were its usual accompaniments. (2) The place of this last awful scene. A considerable literature has in recent years come into existence concerning the site of Calvary. Every Protestant traveler to Jerusalem certainly must wish that the hill above Jeremiah's Grotto is the true site. Scholars are not yet all agreed upon this, but there is a growing consensus in its favor. (See Smith's Hist. Geog., and especially his articles in the " Expositor " [1903] on Jerusalem, where it is to be hoped the question will be fully discussed; see also Stewart's Land of Israel.)

U. Suggestions and Questions for Study. 1. Compare the account critically with that given in the Synoptics, noting all variations. 2. How did two malefactors come to be crucified at the same time? 3. Note how the mockery of Pilate proclaimed to the world the real truth. It is a fine illustration of the unconscious service which evil may render in the plan of God. It is probably because of this fact that John gives this incident of the inscription. 4. With what does "therefore " (23) connect this verse? " The distance of the hill Golgotha from the city, the title upon the cross, the remonstrance of the Jews with Pilate's grim reply, the behavior of the four soldiers on guard, are all told with greater exactness by John than by the Synoptics." 5. How many friends of Jesus stood by the cross, and to what extent were they related (see v. 25)? 6. Why did Jesus commit His mother to the beloved disciple? 7. Was the offering of vinegar a mockery of the Sufferer's thirst? 8. What was finished in the death of Jesus? 9. Why were the legs of the crucified broken? 10. Note the witnesses to the actual death of Jesus— the disciples (25), the Jews (31), indirectly Pilate (31) (see Mark 15 :44, 45), the soldiers (33). Collusion among all these in the attestation of a fact which (according to some modern views) was not a fact is simply impossible. 11. Do the words, "for there are three who bear witness, the spirit and *the water and the blood*" (1 John 5 :8) refer to this scene? Be careful in your answer. 12. Can v. 35 be used as proof that the author distinguishes himself from the apostle? See Godet in loco.

UI. Topic for Research. Did Jesus die of a broken heart? Sufferers by crucifixion have been known to linger as long as seven days. It is certainly remarkable that Jesus died so soon. The student will be interested in reading Stroud's work, entitled, The Physical Cause of Christ's Death.

THE BURIAL. (XIX : 38-42.)

It is interesting to note that at the very moment when unfaith seemed triumphant, faith was exhibited in the persons of two members of the Jewish aristocracy, Joseph and Nicodemus. A sepulchre is shown today in Jerusalem which, if Jeremiah's Grotto was the scene of the crucifixion, meets well the description of John. Thanks to English care, this sepulcher is now in a garden, and in the quiet of its seclusion one may recall the scenes of that evening long ago when sad, faithful friends brought the body of their Lord to its resting place. All had happened as Jesus had predicted. John makes that clear. This supreme hour, which then seemed the very extinguishing of the hopes of the disciples, was to the apostle when he wrote supreme in quite another sense. He has made us see not only the intense perversity of the Jews and the faith of a few trustful souls, but also the total, sublime self-surrender of Him " who died to save us all."

Outline Studies in the Gospel of John,

BY

JAMES STEVENSON RIGGS, D. D.,

Professor of Biblical Criticism in Auburn Theological Seminary, Auburn, N. Y.

Prepared for the Rhode Island Committee of Pastors.

Outline Study XV.

CHAPTERS XX, XXI.

The Resurrection and the Epilogue.

Chapter XX brings before us in John's own way the great subject of the Resurrection. It is questionable whether there is a more important theme for the student of the Gospels than this. Of course, all anti-supernatural theories deny an actual resurrection; that was to be expected, but more serious than this denial is the uncertain tone regarding it heard within the church itself. As in the case of all the miracles of Scripture, philosophic objections and objections based upon the evidence are brought into play. Is a resurrection possible? Was it a fact? Is the physical fact of only subordinate importance as compared with its worth as "a thought of faith" (a Ritschlian conception)? These are some of the questions which press for an answer as soon as one comes to reflect upon this significant theme. We, therefore, take the liberty of pointing out a method of study, indicating at the same time the especial value of John in his testimony. No better order for studying the theme can be given than that given by Paul in the fifteenth chapter of 1 Cor. This order is as follows: (1) The *fact* of the Resurrection and the witnesses thereto; (2) the import and importance of the Resurrection; (3) the manner of the Resurrection; (4) its relation to the believer who has died and to the believer who may be alive when Christ comes again. The points (2), (3), (4), carry us over to the doctrinal significance of this fact, but they all show the supreme importance of the fact itself, and therefore should have careful consideration. The Gospels supply us largely with the facts, and regarding these we wish to emphasize two considerations: (1) The Gospels are not histories in one sense of the word; the variations of personal memories are, therefore, not surprising. It is largely a rigid view of inspiration in some form which stumbles at these variations. An attempted harmonization of them can be gained from any harmony, but it is well always to remember the consideration given above. The *fact* is abundantly testified to by all the sources. The variation in details is explicable from the character of the narrative and from psychological reasons. (2) The second consideration to be emphasized is this: The facts as they are given may be arranged in two series. (*a*) One, to prove that Jesus actually, physically arose from the dead. The empty grave, the taking of food and the witness to Thomas belong in this series. (*b*) The other, to show the typical character of the Resurrection life. It is no longer subject to the same laws as before the Crucifixion. In this series belong the sudden appearances and disappearances. If these two series of facts are kept distinct, the significance of this great fact both for the work of the Messiah and for the resurrection of believers will be apparent. Paul keeps them very carefully apart in his argument for the Corinthians. In John's Gospel we are shown the climacteric manifestation of the Messiah to faith. As usual, the writer gives us only a selected narrative, but its situations are marked by remarkable psychological truthfulness. Professor Sanday's words are not too strong when he says, "We have had before narratives remarkable for beauty and for lifelike minuteness of detail, but here they reach their climax." The chapter, for convenience of study, may be divided into four parts: 1-10, 11-18, 19-23, 24-29, to which is added a conclusion to the whole Gospel in v. 30. Let us look at these in order.

PART I. THE TWO DISCIPLES AT THE GRAVE. (1-10.)

I. Suggestions and Questions for Study. 1. At what point does John begin his narrative, and how is it related to that of the Synoptics? 2. Is Weiss right in supposing that the other women (see Mark 16:1) are not mentioned for the simple reason that it is Mary Magdalene's testimony which interests him? 3. Note the implication of the presence of the other women in "we do not know" (2). 4. If this Gospel was written by John the Presbyter, would he be likely to use such circumlocutions as "the other disciple" (2, 3)? 5. Mark the evidences of an eye-witness in this section. 6. Does the position of the grave-clothes indicate that there had been no grave-robbery? 7. It is well to note how consistently the scripture shows the mental attitude of the disciples toward a resurrection. They were totally unprepared for it, even though Jesus had specifically predicted it. It should also be noted how the light of the Spirit was needed to make the "divine necessity" (9) of it apparent. The disciples had no such knowledge of the Scripture as made them ready for this astounding fact. Also in this section, note carefully how John comes to faith. Godet brings out the force of the confession: "He saw and he believed *at last*." "Perhaps this is the explanation," the commentator adds, "why there is no mention of any particular appearance of the Lord to His beloved disciple, while there is mention of appearance to Peter and James."

PART II. THE APPEARANCE TO MARY MAGDALENE. (11-18.)

II. Suggestions and Questions for Study. 1. Note again that to which we have before referred, that Mary Magdalene was not the kind of woman generally depicted by traditional art. 2. Does this section argue for the reality of angels? 3. Is the failure of Mary to recognize Jesus natural? Does it not from another side argue for the unexpectedness of the Resurrection? This point must have reiterated emphasis. It is simply fatally effective against all visionary hypotheses. 4. The most difficult verse of this section is v. 17, and that in its first part. Several things are to be noted: (*a*) the antithesis is between the verbs "do not touch" and "go"; (*b*) the reason given for the former command is given with a Greek perfect, indicating continued state; (*c*) the first verb in the message she is to give the disciples is to be translated "I am on the point of ascending." The whole passage, therefore, seems to forbid lingering for the purpose of communion. Westcott's translation, "do not now cling to Me," fits to this idea.

PART III. THE APPEARANCE TO THE DISCIPLES, THOMAS BEING ABSENT. (19-23.)

III. Suggestions and Questions for Study. 1. Manifestly we have here in the incident of the "closed doors" a reference to those "supernatural appearances" which were meant to show that Jesus was no longer subject to merely natural conditions. All these incidents should be carefully studied. They present a specific side of the Resurrection life and are doctrinally used by Paul. 2. The exhibition of the hands and side belongs, on the contrary, to the other phase of the Resurrection. They prove that the same body came out of the grave as went into it. Does this signify that our bodies are to be raised at the final resurrection? Answer this question only after studying carefully Paul in 1 Cor. 15:35-50. The fact of Christ's Resurrection should not be used to support incorrect and unscriptural doctrines. 3. What is the force of "even so" in v. 21? 4. Just what did Jesus mean by "receive (the) Holy Spirit"? Does it anticipate Pentecost? 5. Interpret the latter part of v. 23. Has the power of "forgiving sins" ever been actually given to men?

PART IV. THE APPEARANCE TO THOMAS. (24-29.)

As introductory to the study of this scene, two points are noteworthy: (1) Doubt has its source either in the will or in the reason. With wilful doubt Jesus had little sympathy; with doubt of the reason he was always patient, tender and helpful. (2) The confession of Thomas brings the Gospel to an end upon the high plane on which it began. "Thou art my Lord and my *God.*" "In the beginning was the Word."

TU. Suggestions and Questions for Study. 1. Note how consistent with all we know from other scenes this portrayal of Thomas is. 2. The form of the conditional sentence (25) in the Greek reveals the mental attitude of Thomas. It virtually says: "Give me *facts* and I, too, will believe." 3. Note that the faith of Thomas requires more for its explanation than the physical evidence. That was but the *occasion;* the cause lay deeper. 4. The work of the Master recorded in the Synoptics is certainly allowed for in v. 30. The purpose of the Gospel, as we have often emphasized, is given in v. 31.

U. Topic for Research. How would you meet the position that if the Spirit of Christ lived on, a resurrection was not necessary.

THE EPILOGUE.

Chapter XXI.

The heading of this part of our study indicates a judgment upon the character of this chapter. Two questions present themselves regarding it and they have been each variously answered. (1) Is this chapter really an epilogue? (2) By whom was it written? There is by no means such difference of opinion in regard to the first question as in regard to the second. Space is not afforded us here to give the arguments on each side. We must refer the student to Weiss (Com. on John) for the defence of the view that the chapter was written by another hand, and to Godet for the argument supporting Johannine authorship. Slight variations in language are certainly well offset by these marks of psychological fidelity which are everywhere in this gospel worthy of careful attention. Vs. 24, 25 are unquestionably by another hand. To this same hand Weiss attributes the composition of the entire chapter and he appeals to v. 2 for a confirmation of his view. On the other hand see the familiar designation in v. 20. The purpose of this addition to the gospel is clearly to prevent a misunderstanding of the words of Jesus and is given in v. 23. It had been commonly understood that Jesus had said that John would live until He came again. This verse is to show that Jesus spoke only hypothetically "if I will &c." The chapter for convenience of study falls naturally into three parts. 1. The miraculous draught of fishes (1-14). 2. Prophecies concerning Peter and John (15-23). 3. The closing words (24, 25).

PART I. THE MIRACULOUS DRAUGHT OF FISHES. (1-14.)

The opinion of Weiss that in Luke 5 we have an anticipated account of an event which John gives in the right place deserves critical attention. The student should endeavor to see whether the narrative as given by John has a more intelligible connection and reason than in the position given by Luke. Precisely the same kind of question appears here as in reference to the proper place for the story of the Cleansing of the Temple. The disciples had gone back to their old homes. They were once more at their old occupation when Jesus appeared to them. It is in the words to Peter that the author sees the importance of this story.

UI. Questions and Suggestions for Study. 1. By what different names is the Lake of Galilee known? 1. Do you see in the expression "the sons of Zebedee" an evidence of "another hand" in this chapter? It is interesting to note that it is used to confirm directly opposite opinions. 3. Godet calls attention in each verse to the marks of Johannine style. It were well to note them. 4. Observe the delicate touches revealing the character of the two apostles (7, 8). 5. To which of the series of post-resurrection facts does the incident of 9-13 belong? 5. Should the whole story be given a symbolical meaning, as intended by the writer? 6. Especially is a question of this kind in order in reference to the number 153? Has this any other significance than to confirm the eye-witness character of the narrative? Would not such a catch lead to this very numbering to mark how great it was? 7. Is the expression " this is now the third time " meant to correct the synoptical narrative? 8. Has this scene for its prime purpose the proof of the Resurrection, or does it serve another object? What is that object?

PART II. THE PROPHECIES CONCERNING PETER AND JOHN.

(15-23).

VII. Questions and Suggestions for Study. 1. This section should be kept in close parallel with Peter's denials in order to get its full force. 2. Should "these" (15) be referred to the disciples or to the paraphernalia of the fishing business? 3. Is Godet right in emphasizing the difference between the two Greek verbs expressing love used all through this section? 4. Are the terms "feed," "shepherd," expressive of a peculiar work assigned to Peter? Do this passage and Matt. 16: 18 confer a primacy of any kind upon Peter? Does v. 18 indicate any more than a violent death or does it specifically point to crucifixion? 6. Interpret fully the words "follow me" *i. e.* give the spiritual equivalent of the spatial direction. 7. Note the specific personal marks given in 20. 8. Do you see in Peter's question (21) a wrong motive? 9. Does Godet's interpretation by which he refuses to find in the "if I will" of Jesus (22) a mere supposition, appear to you to be correct? Note the conclusion to which it leads this commentator.

PART III. THE CONCLUDING VERSES.

VIII. Questions and Suggestions for Study. 1. Might John the Presbyter be the disciple who wrote these verses? 2. Who are included in the oidamen? 3. Does v. 25 confirm the general view that our gospels are only memorabilia. You will recall that Jesus speaks of the wonderful works done in Bethsaida and Chorazin. We have no record of one of them. Of course the statement in v. 25 is an oriental exaggeration.

Our study of this noble gospel has come to an end. To that study which makes experience, life the chief interpreter, there can never be an end. It calls us to go on to know the Lord through all the profound realities of communion and obedience which involve the ultimate depths of life. The deeper we go by this way of interpretation the surer shall we be that this is no fabricated portrait of the Master. It is rather the picture of one who saw not merely the scenery of Galilee and Judea; nor simply the external forms of that memorable group now known as Master and Disciples, but whose profoundly religious spirit, touched, illumined, guided by the Spirit of Truth, grasped the eternal significance of Him to whom his life had been given. Is there a subjective element in John? Of course there is, but it is the subjectivism of one whose insight was directed to the inner, eternal meanings of Jesus. Rightly has it been said that John saw Jesus and His truth *sub specie Eternitatis.* Does that make the gospel less true? Evidence enough there is of its historicity. No other gospel is more faithful to historical situations; no other gospel is more keenly alive to psychological presentations. Its portraiture of Jesus, different as is its setting from that of the synoptics, is thoroughly consistent with theirs. What they exhibit constantly in action and now and then by word is here completely interpreted in that blaze of glory which casts a noon-day clearness upon the person and character of the Messiah.

www.ingramcontent.com/pod-product-compliance
Lightning Source LLC
Chambersburg PA
CBHW022145090426
42742CB00010B/1393